AMERICA'S FORGOTTEN FOUNDERS

LIVES OF THE FOUNDERS

EDITED BY JOSIAH BUNTING III

AMERICA'S FORGOTTEN FOUNDERS

SECOND EDITION

*Edited by Gary L. Gregg II
and Mark David Hall*

REGNERY GATEWAY
Washington, D.C.

Originally published by the Intercollegiate Studies Institute

The chapter "Famous Founders and Forgotten Founders: What's the Difference, and Does the Difference Matter?" was originally published as "Founders Famous and Forgotten" in the *Intercollegiate Review* 42 (Fall 2007), 3–12. It has been revised for this volume.

Regnery Gateway™ is a trademark of Salem Communications Holding Corporation
Regnery® is a registered trademark and its colophon is a trademark of Salem Communications Holding Corporation

Cataloging-in-Publication data on file with the Library of Congress

ISBN: 9781610170239
eISBN: 9781684516025

Published in the United States by
Regnery Gateway, an Imprint of
Regnery Publishing
A Division of Salem Media Group
Washington, D.C.
www.Regnery.com

Manufactured in the United States of America

2023 Printing

To Mitch McConnell and Elaine L. Chao

—GLG

To Uncle Wayne and Aunt Sally

—MDH

CONTENTS

INTRODUCTION

GARY L. GREGG II and MARK DAVID HALL

WHEN AMERICANS THINK OF THE FOUNDING FATHERS, ONLY A handful of leaders generally come to mind. Although the list may vary slightly from person to person, names like Benjamin Franklin, George Washington, John Adams, Thomas Jefferson, James Madison, and Alexander Hamilton inevitably surface. In some respects this is not surprising given that by any measure these statesmen are among the most important and influential men in American history. A narrow focus on these great men, however, does not tell the full story of the American Founding experience and can be misleading in several ways:

(1) It is tempting to generalize from these six men to all of the Founders, but it is not self-evident that their views represent those held by all Founders. Indeed, our own research indicates that at least in some cases they do not.

(2) As with most history, the list is biased toward "winners." Some men and women on the losing side of important debates and actions—such as the declaration of American independence

and the ratification of the U.S. Constitution—made significant contributions to America's Founding.

(3) The list may be biased in terms of race and gender. Even acknowledging the cultural facts of the period, there is no denying that there were women and racial minorities who played significant, if largely unrecognized, roles in the overall events that comprise the American Founding.

(4) The list favors men who served prominently in the executive branch of government. It is noteworthy that four of the six most readily recognizable Founders served as president of the United States of America.

Daniel L. Dreisbach, in this volume's lead essay, addresses the question of why some Founders are remembered and others are not. He argues that, in general, the famous Founders were recognized as great in their own day, came from power centers in the new nation, supported the Declaration of Independence and/or the new Constitution, left a voluminous paper trail, and (with the exception of Franklin) played prominent roles in the new national government. He does not suggest that the famous Founders were not great men, but he does contend that there is "a much larger company of statesmen who made salient contributions in thought, word, and deed to the construction of America's republican institutions." We agree.

In order to promote study of a wider range of Founders, we asked more than one hundred history, political science, and law professors who have written on the Founding era to respond to the following question:

Who are the Founders that have been neglected in American history texts and in public knowledge but who played significant enough roles to be remembered or whose example and thought should be remembered in America today?

For the purpose of the survey, we defined "Founders" as "the broad group of men and women who helped secure America's independence from Great Britain and/or helped establish the new constitutional republic and its political institutions." These individuals may or may not have held political office, and in some instances they may have even been on the "losing" side of history with respect to some issues.

Our respondents listed seventy-three men and women who they believed have been unjustly neglected by history. The complete list is found in Appendix B at the back of this volume.

We were surprised and encouraged by the wide range of names suggested by our respondents. Their responses raise a number of questions, but none more intriguing than "Who should count as a Founder?" For instance, should Founders include men and women such as:

Nancy Ward/Nanye-hi (c. 1738–1822), a female Cherokee leader who advocated peaceful coexistence with whites.

George Whitefield (1714–1770), the English minister whose preaching tours of America helped spark the First Great Awakening (1730s–1740s).

Phillis Wheatley (1753–1784), the African American poet who was born into slavery.

John Marshall (1755–1835), the great chief justice whose primary contributions to the creation of the American Republic were made after 1800.

Ezra Stiles (1727–1795), the Congregationalist clergyman and president of Yale College who never held a political office.

The diversity reflected in the list of Founders produced by our survey points to the difficulty scholars have in untangling the extremely complex web of events and personalities that make up any human endeavor, particularly one from a distant past. Who can really account for the importance of the whispered word of advice on some late night after the children have gone off to bed or the chance meeting of men in an inn the night before a key decision would be made? Who can truly understand the ultimate impact of any one man or woman and how history might have been different if they had not lived or engaged in the world of affairs? We appreciate the efforts of our survey participants to untangle some of history's webs.

Without discounting the value of considering a wide range of individuals, for the purposes of this survey we wanted to see whether scholars could agree on a short list of important but neglected Founders. Accordingly, we submitted to the original group of acadmics the names of the thirty Founders who were mentioned most often in the first round of our survey. We asked these historians, political scientists, and law professors to rank the top ten Founders in this group in order of importance. In making this request, we acknowledged that "'importance' is not easily quantifiable" but stipulated that "we are interested to see if a general consensus emerges as to the top tier of forgotten Founders."

The respondents ranked Founders on a scale of one to ten, with one being the most important. We weighted each vote, assigning ten points for a first-place vote, nine for a second-place vote, etc. We then calculated the number of points received by each forgotten Founder. The Pennsylvania Scot James Wilson received the most points by a significant margin, making us wonder why he is not better known among the general public. Indeed, he outpolled arguably better-known men such as George Mason, Patrick Henry, and Thomas Paine by huge margins.

The consensus top ten Founders, according to our survey, are:

Rank	Founder	Points
1	James Wilson	214
2	George Mason	152
3	Gouverneur Morris	128
4	John Jay	125
5	Roger Sherman	124
6	John Marshall	117
7	John Dickinson	92
8	Thomas Paine	76
9	Patrick Henry	71
10	John Witherspoon	68

After Witherspoon, the total number of points for each Founder begins to drop precipitously. For instance, the lowest ten vote recipients received a total of 103 points, fewer points than any of the first six forgotten Founders received by himself. The complete list of thirty finalists in order of points received may be found in Appendix B.

Before we proceed, two caveats are in order. First, we would like to emphasize that we are not arguing that we have "scientifically" determined a list of Founders who deserve to be added to the pantheon of famous elites. We do think, however, it is interesting that there is a clear consensus among experts on the era about a relatively short list of significant but neglected Founders. By any measure, each of the ten men on our list played an important role in either the Revolution or the creation of the American Republic, and five of them were significantly involved in both.

Second, we recognize that one might object that John Marshall is neither "forgotten" nor a "Founder." Certainly he is reasonably well known—although not nearly as famous as the six most recognizable Founders. More significant is the complaint that he should not be considered a Founder because his primary contributions were made after 1800. Although he served the Revolution and Virginia's ratifying convention, if he had died in 1800 there is no chance he would be on our list of forgotten Founders. Nevertheless, because we defined Founders as "the broad group of men and women who helped . . . establish the new constitutional republic and its political institutions," it is reasonable to view him as playing a critical role in this enterprise.

It is noteworthy that none of our top ten forgotten Founders played a significant role in the executive branch of the national government (although Marshall served as secretary of state for almost a year, and Morris was minister plenipotentiary to France from 1792 to 1794). Sherman and Marshall served briefly in the House of Representatives, and Sherman and Morris were United States senators. Although Wilson, Jay, and Marshall all served on the Supreme Court, only Marshall can lay claim to making a significant impact from the bench. With the exception of Marshall, none of these men played a "prominent" role in the new national government. Indeed, five of our forgotten Founders died before 1800. Thus, there is a striking difference between our list here and that of the most recognizable six figures. It says something about how the establishment of the new government after 1787 is treated in our history books compared with the period of preparation immediately preceding it.

Each of the top ten forgotten Founders was reasonably well known in the Founding era, and most of them were well regarded for their mastery of the written or spoken word. However, none left an extensive collection of papers. The papers of Marshall, Paine, and Witherspoon have been published in twelve, ten, and nine volumes, respectively. Otherwise, papers of these forgotten Founders have been published in collections ranging between one and four volumes—if they have been published at all. By contrast, George Washington's papers are projected to fill ninety volumes, the Adams family papers one hundred, Jefferson's will run approximately seventy-five, and the James Madison and Benjamin Franklin papers projects are expected to contain at least fifty volumes.

Each of our top forgotten Founders was on the "winning side" of history, with three minor exceptions. John Dickinson famously refused to vote for the Declaration of Independence but supported the War for Independence in a variety of other ways, and he later helped draft and supported the U.S. Constitution. George Mason and Patrick Henry, on the other hand, were ardent supporters of the Revolution, but each opposed the adoption of the Constitution.

It is striking that three of our top forgotten Founders—James Wilson, John Witherspoon, and Thomas Paine—were recent immigrants, as was one of the most famous Founders, Alexander Hamilton. Moreover, each of these men, as well as Roger Sherman, John Marshall, and the famous Founder Benjamin Franklin, were from humble backgrounds. None of these individuals was born into abject poverty, but neither did they come from wealthy, established families. Unlike the Old World, America provided room for a variety of bright, hard-working (white) men to become important civic leaders.

Many readers of this work are undoubtedly familiar with most of the names on our list of forgotten Founders, but even specialists in the Founding era may not be able to explain why each of these individuals is significant. Accordingly, we have commissioned profiles of our top ten forgotten Founders. We hope these profiles encourage study and discussion of a wide range of Founders, but we do not think that the expanded discussion should be limited to them. Following these profiles, we offer a brief discussion of America's other forgotten Founders.

FAMOUS FOUNDERS AND FORGOTTEN FOUNDERS
What's the Difference, and Does the Difference Matter?

DANIEL L. DREISBACH

CONSIDER THE POLITICAL CAREER OF ROGER SHERMAN (1721–1793) of Connecticut, a largely self-taught man, devout Calvinist, and lifelong public servant. He was one of only two men who signed the three great expressions of American organic law: the Declaration of Independence, the Articles of Confederation, and the U.S. Constitution.[1] He was a delegate to the First and Second Continental Congresses (serving longer than all but four men),[2] a member of the five-man committee formed to draft the Declaration of Independence, and a member of the committee of thirteen formed to frame the Articles of Confederation. At the federal Constitutional Convention of 1787, he delivered more speeches than all but three delegates and was a driving force behind the Great (Connecticut) Compromise. He was a member of the first U.S. House of Representatives (1789–1791) and later the U.S. Senate (1791–1793), where he played key roles in deliberations on the Bill of Rights, the elimination of accumulated state debts, and the creation of a national bank. If any man merits the mantle of "Founding Father," it is Roger Sherman. Yet few Americans recall, let alone mention, Sherman's name when enumerating the Founding Fathers; even among those familiar with his name, most would be hard-pressed to describe Sherman's role in the Founding. Why is it that a man of such prodigious contributions to the new nation is today an all but forgotten figure? The same question could be asked about many other Patriots—John Dickinson, Elbridge Gerry, John Jay, Richard Henry Lee, George Mason, Gouverneur Morris, Charles Pinckney, Benjamin Rush, John Rutledge, James Wilson, and John Witherspoon, just to name a few—who labored diligently to establish an independent American republic.

When asked to identify the "Founding Fathers," Americans typically respond with a short list of a half dozen or so notables who have achieved iconic status in the American imagination and collective memory. This is true of even serious students of American history. The small fraternity of "famous Founders" typically includes (in no particular order) Benjamin Franklin, George Washington, John Adams, Thomas Jefferson, James Madison, and Alexander Hamilton. To this short list, individual historians occasionally add a favorite figure or two.[3]

There is, however, a much larger company of statesmen who made salient contributions in thought, word, and deed to the construction of America's republican institutions. Unfortunately, many among the Founding generation whose contributions and sacrifices were consequential in the creation of a new nation have slipped into unmerited obscurity, wrested from the elite fraternity of famous Founders. Why are some individuals whose well-documented contributions were valued by their peers and celebrated in their time largely forgotten in our time? In short, why are a few Founders "famous" and others now "forgotten"?

A preliminary question pertinent to this discussion is, who is a Founding Father? Whose thoughts, words, and/or deeds qualify one to be called a Founding Father? Historians have long debated this question. A common, but narrow, construction of the term limits membership in the fraternity of Founding Fathers to the approximately 120 men who signed the Declaration of Independence (1776), Articles of Confederation (drafted 1777, signed 1778, and ratified 1781), and/or U.S. Constitution (drafted and signed 1787 and ratified 1788).[4] Nothing like a verifiable presence at the creation confers on one a plausible claim to immortality as a Founding Father. This narrow definition, however, excludes Patrick Henry, Thomas Paine, John Jay, and John Marshall, among other prominent Patriots. The term could be construed more broadly to include a generation or two of Americans from many walks of life who in the last half of the eighteenth century and early nineteenth century articulated the rights of colonists, secured independence from Great Britain, and established the new constitutional republic and its political institutions. Among them were citizen soldiers, elected representatives, polemicists, and clergymen. This definition of the Founders includes members of the Stamp Act Congress; Continental and Confederation Congresses; state legislative bodies of the period that debated and declared independence, drafted state constitutions and declarations of rights, deliberated the structure of a national union, and ratified the U.S. Constitution; Constitutional Convention of 1787; and early federal Congresses under the U.S. Constitution (especially the First Congress, which framed the national Bill of Rights). This expansive definition includes a cast of thousands who played their patriotic part at the local, state, and/or national levels.

WHY ARE SOME FOUNDERS FAMOUS?

Before we consider why some important Founders are now forgotten, it is worth asking why the famous Founders are famous.
Do they share characteristics or experiences that explain their
prominence or separate them from lesser-known Founders? There
is no single factor or set of factors that satisfactorily explains why
selected Founders are famous or forgotten. Rather, a variety of factors and circumstances helps explain why certain Founders have
been placed in the pantheon of famous Founders and others have
slipped into unmerited obscurity.

The lists today of famous Founders almost always include
Franklin, Washington, Adams, Jefferson, Madison, and Hamilton. But has the fraternity of famous Founders always been limited
to this select group? The popularly accepted list of famous Founders, one writer has recently argued, has not been static during the
past two hundred years. The generation that lived through the
American War of Independence venerated and celebrated military
heroes, men such as George Washington (always first), Nathanael
Greene, Henry Knox, and even the Marquis de Lafayette. Americans in the early nineteenth century placed the mantle of greatness
on the "host of worthies," as Jefferson called them, who framed and
signed the Declaration of Independence.[5] These men are depicted
in John Trumbull's iconic 12-by-18-foot oil painting "Declaration
of Independence" (commissioned in 1817), which now hangs in the
Rotunda of the U.S. Capitol and is memorialized on the back of
the two-dollar note.[6] Later generations counted among the Founding Fathers the "assembly of demigods" (again, to use Jefferson's
phrase) who crafted a new national Constitution in the summer
of 1787.[7]

Those recognized today as famous Founders have not always been assured a seat in this elite company. Merrill D. Peterson in *The Jefferson Image in the American Mind* and, more recently, Stephen F. Knott in *Alexander Hamilton and the Persistence of Myth* track the rise and fall of Jefferson's and Hamilton's respective standings in the public mind. "Alexander Hamilton's place at any period on the imaginary scale that charts American reputations is always a good index to Jefferson's," Peterson observed.[8] At different moments in history, for a variety of political reasons, Jefferson's stature waxed as Hamilton's waned, and at other times the opposite was true.[9] Only a recent bestselling biography of John Adams by David McCullough, commentators have remarked with perhaps slight exaggeration, reinstated the irascible Bay Stater among the famous Founders.[10] Thus, if the past is a reliable guide, future generations may celebrate selected Founders for still other reasons—perhaps including women whose contributions have been largely ignored in the standard histories or honoring those who opposed slavery at a time when it was not always popular to do so. All this suggests the fluid nature of membership in the exclusive fraternity of famous Founders.

It is worth noting that Benjamin Franklin was, at one point, the most famous American in the Western world, celebrated widely as much for his scientific achievements as for his political contributions to the American cause. This was a remarkable achievement for a "colonial." And by the time independence from Great Britain was secured, George Washington was, perhaps, equally famous. Their celebrated status at home and abroad went far in securing their place in the pantheon of famous Founders. Despite the vagaries of politics and fashion, Franklin and Washington, unlike all other Founders, have never had their status as top-tier Founders seriously questioned or challenged in the past two centuries, at least not in popular discourse.[11]

Fame is not easily manufactured. "[T]he great whom the present recognizes," Robert G. McCloskey observed, "tend to be those who were thought of as great in their time. Tomorrow may enhance or diminish yesterday's reputation; it does not often create a wholly new one."[12] Every Founder who has resided at one point or another in the upper echelon of Founders was recognized in his day by his peers as worthy of fame; Founders whose contemporaries—those who knew them personally—were reluctant to place the mantle of fame and greatness upon them have not risen above that initial, critical assessment in the public imagination.[13]

Students of the American Founding know well that many Founders—none more so than the elite famous Founders—were extraordinarily attentive to their place in history. The notoriously vain John Adams frequently fretted about whether he would receive the recognition he rightly deserved.[14] In his final winter, Thomas Jefferson beseeched his Virginia neighbor James Madison to "[t]ake care of me when dead."[15] The Founding generation was acutely aware that they had been present at the creation of something remarkable in human history. With an awareness of posterity's judgment, many recorded their recollections in contemporaneous journals and correspondence or later in memoirs. The famous Founders recognized the historical value of their papers and went to great lengths to preserve them.

Some of this behavior appears to be vain, petty jockeying for a preferred position in posterity. But was it? What did fame and the pursuit of fame mean to this generation of Americans? In his now classic essay "Fame and the Founding Fathers," historian Douglass Adair argued that the Founders' "obsessive desire for fame" was not merely a vain or vulgar quest for celebrity, popularity, or deification by their countrymen.[16] Rather, for this generation, steeped in the classical tradition, fame was akin to what we might call honor, virtue, and good reputation. Indeed, there were, in this sense, few higher callings than the pursuit of fame.

"The love of honest and well earned fame," James Wilson remarked, "is deeply rooted in honest and susceptible minds."[17] "[T]he love of fame [is] the ruling passion of the noblest minds," wrote Alexander Hamilton in the *Federalist Papers*.[18] As with the Romans, the Founders thought fame meant placing duty to one's home and country above one's personal interests. Great men earned true fame by curbing selfish appetites and wanton emotion and by performing acts of uncommon virtue and patriotism that promoted the commonwealth. "The love of fame," Hamilton reported, "would prompt a man to plan and undertake extensive and arduous enterprises for the public benefit."[19] Yes, fame is very much concerned with immortality, and, yes, "the greatest of the great generation" of Founders became obsessively "concerned with posterity's judgment of their behavior." For the less noble among them, the love and pursuit of fame could be an idol, and unchecked ambition could be a dangerous vice. Yet, as Adair observed, "[t]he audience that men who desire Fame are incited to act before is the audience of the wise and the good in the future— that part of posterity that can discriminate between virtue and vice—that audience that can recognize egotism transmuted gloriously into public service." The passion for fame "can spur individuals to spend themselves to provide for the common defense, or to promote the general welfare, and even on occasion to establish justice in a world where justice is extremely rare." For the noble man, fame was a desirable incentive to pursue right principles and worthy objectives. The pursuit of fame, Adair continued, "thus transmuted the leaden desire for self-aggrandizement and personal reward into a golden concern for public service and the promotion of the commonwealth as the means to gain glory."[20] Fame, the Founders were taught, was the spur that goaded men to live lives of honor, virtue, and personal sacrifice.

What, then, makes a Founder famous? All the famous Founders had strong, memorable, and (with the possible exception of Madison) colorful personalities. All came from and represented influential power centers in the new nation. None came from a small or isolated corner of the union. All, it goes without saying, made significant and enduring contributions to the *national* polity in the critical years between the formation of the Continental Congress and the establishment of the national government under the Constitution. All except Franklin (who died in 1790) played a prominent role on the national political stage following implementation of the U.S. Constitution (indeed, four of the six famous Founders became president). Throughout their adult lives, they were consistent and unceasing in their commitment to the American cause, rarely deviating to pursue ventures in other venues; and in retirement they could reflect upon, as did George Washington in his Farewell Address (1796), "forty five years of my life dedicated to its [my Country's] Service, with an upright zeal."[21] All were acutely aware of their place in history and took steps to ensure that their contributions would be remembered and to shape how their contributions would be remembered by future generations. All left a voluminous paper trail of public and private documents that provided historians with a record of their deeds and insights into their views and actions. They were not only prolific writers, but also all masters of the written word. Even Washington, often dismissed as an inferior wordsmith, could be surprisingly eloquent in both the spoken and the written word.

These are the characteristics of the famous Founders.

WHY ARE SOME FOUNDERS FORGOTTEN?

Many of these characteristics and achievements also describe selected forgotten Founders. So what explains why some Founders are famous and others not? Again, there are a variety of factors distinguishing the famous from the not-so-famous Founders, and, to some extent, each Founder must be individually examined. A unique combination of factors and circumstances explains why some figures have not been duly recognized by history. That said, a number of factors are recurring features in the lives of Founders relegated to obscurity.

Age (or generational factors) and time of death may explain why some viable candidates for top-tier status are now largely forgotten. With the exception of Franklin, who died in 1790, all the famous Founders went on to distinguished careers in national politics under the U.S. Constitution, whereas some important forgotten Founders, such as William Livingston (1723–1790), George Mason (1725–1792), John Hancock (1737–1793), Roger Sherman (1721–1793), Richard Henry Lee (1732–1794), and John Witherspoon (1723–1794), died in the early 1790s without playing a prominent role in the new national government under the Constitution. These men, for the most part, were of a slightly older generation than the famous Founders (with the exception of Franklin). For example, George Mason, born in 1725, was seven years older than his neighbor and lifelong friend George Washington. He was a decade older than John Adams, eighteen years older than Thomas Jefferson, twenty-six years older than James Madison, and thirty or so years older than Alexander Hamilton.

A failure to play a prominent role on the national political stage after the Constitution's implementation may have denied some otherwise worthy Patriots seats in the Founders hall of fame. Their reasons for not taking to this stage are legion: death, retirement from public life, a focus on state or local politics, or the pursuit of other ventures such as business or the law. Fame has been especially elusive for those who channeled their energies into state and local politics following the bitter battles of the independence struggle, even though they were no less passionate about public service and the cause of American liberty than their more famous compatriots. In any case, their departure from the national political scene at the very moment when prominent colleagues were taking leading roles on the newly available national stage undoubtedly contributed to their disappearance from public memory.

Fame has not smiled on Founders of few words or those who left an insufficient paper trail to inform or interest historians. There must be enough of an extant record with which students of history can work. A written record or historical narrative is vital for duly crediting a Founder for his contributions. With considerable discomfort, Madison scribbled transcripts and copious notes of proceedings in the Constitutional Convention that, not surprisingly, recorded his contributions in a favorable light and ensured his place in history.[22] All the famous Founders left enough words that, even two hundred years after their demise, archivists still labor to collect and transcribe their papers, filling many scores of published volumes.[23] Of particular value to historians are letters, journals, and diaries, which give an account of an individual's day-to-day activities, often provide a measure of a man's character, and open a window into his motivations and aspirations. ("Without Jefferson's letters," Gordon S. Wood asked, "what would we know of his mind?")[24]

The papers that were preserved and later archived and, still later, published reflected evolving private and public perceptions of whose contributions were consequential and, thus, whose papers were worthy of preservation for future generations. An individual Founder's decision to keep a journal, write a memoir or autobiography, or preserve correspondence or other documents was an initial self-assessment of that Founder's contribution to some event or desire to memorialize his or her role in history. Subsequent decisions made by family, acquaintances, or executors to preserve or discard such documents after an individual's death were, similarly, a pivotal assessment as to whether the deceased's activities were noteworthy. Even before some had died, family members and others in society recognized the importance of preserving papers associated with particular Founders. Unfortunately, the same generation failed to appreciate the value of other Founders' papers, and thus many were lost to history. Decisions of still later historians and archivists to preserve and publish a Founder's papers reified earlier decisions regarding which Founders are notable and which are not. Major papers publication projects sponsored by universities and historical societies and funded by government initiatives and private foundations seemingly confirmed that the subjects of these projects were the truly consequential Founders. A fresh review of history might well lead one to conclude that previously discounted or discarded papers of certain forgotten Founders would be invaluable to a well-rounded understanding of the American Founding. Regrettably, however, decisions and accompanying actions made at various points in the preceding two centuries have made it exceedingly difficult, if not impossible, to re-create the historical record. More important, the steps taken long ago to preserve or discard historical documents have shaped how subsequent scholars have assessed the thoughts, words, and deeds of the Founders.

George Mason of Virginia and John Witherspoon of New Jersey are examples of Founders whose reputations may have been diminished in subsequent historical accounts because of gaps in the relevant documentary records. Mason, the principal draftsman of the influential Virginia Declaration of Rights (1776) and among the most voluble members of the Constitutional Convention, is survived by a dearth of papers, which have been collected in a mere three volumes.[25] As his first major biographer observed in the late nineteenth century, "His life never having been written, his papers having been lost and scattered," it is, perhaps, no wonder that "justice has not been done to George Mason." Mason's biographers, unlike Washington's, Jefferson's, and Madison's, have not had their subject's extensive recollections and papers "before them" in which the subject's leading role in legislative deliberations "is chiefly dwelt on" and emphasized.[26] Then there is the case of the Reverend Doctor John Witherspoon, a signer of the Declaration of Independence and Articles of Confederation and an active member of more than 120 committees in the Continental Congress. In Witherspoon's case, the problem is not the lack of papers; rather, it concerns copious papers that were lost or destroyed. Nine volumes of his collected works were published very early in the nineteenth century, but many of these papers pertained to his European career, and the published collection was out of print and exceedingly difficult to find for much of the past two centuries. More important, despite devoting two days per week in his later years to correspondence, only a handful of his many letters survive. The loss of so many primary documents giving insight into his political thought and actions at a critical time in the nation's history is due, among other reasons, to the sacking of the College of New Jersey's Nassau Hall and president's home following the Battle of Princeton and to Witherspoon's instructions shortly before his death to burn many of his papers.[27] Unlike Franklin, Adams, Jefferson, and Madison, neither Mason nor Witherspoon wrote an autobiography or left a journal or diary that might have given succeeding generations a revealing self-portrait of his character, motives, and achievements and, perhaps, enhanced his standing in history. The paper trails left by a host of other Founders are even more meager than those left by Mason and Witherspoon. History might well have been written differently had important figures such as Gerry, Henry, Jay, Randolph, Sherman, and Wilson left more papers, both public and private, for scrutiny by later generations.

Fame has often accompanied men, especially political leaders, eloquent in spoken word. The Founders lived in an age in which political power and influence were often derived from and defined by oratorical prowess. (Contemporaneous biographical sketches of the Founders frequently remarked on the subject's public-speaking skills as if they were a measure of that figure's greatness.) Patrick Henry, for example, was greatly admired in his time, and is remembered today, for his matchless gifts of oratory. James Madison, by contrast, had a weak voice and a diffident disposition, which seem for a time to have impeded justly deserved recognition and diminished his public standing. In short, men of great minds but weak elocution often are not duly appreciated in their own time. The Founders' literal voices have long been silenced, and all that remains are their written words. There is some irony in the fact that, although masters of the *spoken* word may have garnered more power and acclaim in their own day, today the masters of the *written* word are more celebrated.

According to a well-worn axiom, history is written by the victors. The reputations of several important Founders have been damaged, one suspects, because they were on the losing side of great debates or controversies, especially the bitter debates over the declaration of American independence and ratification of the proposed national constitution. Consider, for example, John Dickinson of Delaware and Pennsylvania (serving both states as the elected chief executive), who championed the cause of American liberties in his brilliant series *Letters from a Farmer in Pennsylvania* (1767–1768) and who was a delegate to the Stamp Act Congress, where he drafted the Declaration of Rights and Grievances (October 1765); a member of the First and Second Continental Congresses, where he was the principal draftsman of the Declaration of the Causes and Necessity of Taking Up Arms (July 6, 1775); and one of Delaware's delegates to the Constitutional Convention of 1787. In 1776, however, he spoke eloquently against and refused to sign the Declaration of Independence because he thought it premature and intemperate, and his reputation and public career suffered for it, despite commendable subsequent service to the nation. It has been said of George Mason that "[h]is opposition to ratification of the federal Constitution—a document whose shape he helped mightily to craft—started his fall from the national memory."[28] The public standing of other vocal critics of the proposed Constitution was arguably diminished by their controversial stances in this most important national debate, despite the fact that some later became ardent admirers of the charter. Among the critics were Patrick Henry, Richard Henry Lee, Elbridge Gerry, Samuel Adams, George Clinton, Luther Martin, and John Francis Mercer. Other Founders may have similarly fallen from public favor because of their advocacy of positions and causes that later proved unpopular.

The stature of some Founders has risen and fallen with the vagaries of subsequent politics. As political parties emerged in the late eighteenth century and carved out well-defined identities in the nineteenth century, partisans often appropriated selected Founders as precursor spokesmen for or ideological models of their party perspectives, or as avowed opponents of some partisan position. The Jacksonian Democrats of the 1820s and succeeding decades, for example, described themselves as inheritors of the Jeffersonian tradition and demonized Federalist Party stalwarts, such as Alexander Hamilton, John Adams (an especially inviting target because his son John Quincy Adams was Andrew Jackson's immediate foe), and John Marshall, for their opposition to Jeffersonian politics.[29] (The reputations of other prominent Federalists—such as Fisher Ames, John Jay, Rufus King, Gouverneur Morris, and C. C. Pinckney—may have similarly suffered in the wake of their party's demise and Republican ascendancy at the turn of the century.) Thus, Jefferson's reputation as a Founder flourished and Federalist Founders' reputations floundered as Jacksonianism ascended. The War Between the American States and its aftermath prompted a reappraisal of Hamilton's staunch advocacy of a strong national government, and, in the North at least, Hamilton eclipsed the states-rights Jefferson as a "revered figure in the minds of most Americans."[30] According to Merrill D. Peterson, "Jefferson's reputation merely survived the War; Hamilton's was remade by it."[31] In summary, political partisans of succeeding generations have promoted or demoted selected Founders in the public mind depending on whether a Founder's views and associations advanced or impeded respectively the goals of these latter-day partisans.

Another explanation focuses on certain Founders' unappealing personal traits, quirks, or eccentricities, or alleged moral failings. George Mason's truculent temperament and general aversion to public life almost certainly diminished his profile in the history of the Founding era. He was a most reluctant public figure. Mason seems to have been unconcerned about his place in the history books, eschewing the limelight and declining to pursue high office (although reluctantly accepting public office when called).

An abrasive, egotistical personality did little to enhance Thomas Paine's reputation, and pious Americans from his day to the present have reviled him for his assaults on Christianity. John Adams described the radical pamphleteer as "the lying rascal," and Teddy Roosevelt denounced him as that "filthy little atheist."[32] And so the most influential polemicist of the age, renowned on both sides of the Atlantic, died in relative obscurity in 1809 without a eulogy from his former compatriots in the struggle for American independence. Gouverneur Morris's well-earned reputation as a profligate rake and lecher may have diminished his standing among prudish nineteenth-century Americans. In a very different vein, Aaron Burr's widely publicized roguish, even "murderous" and allegedly treasonous, conduct has kept him alive in the public memory, but it almost certainly has demoted him from the pedestal of a venerated Founder. There is the tragic case of James Wilson, who died in ignominy in 1798 at age fifty-five, fleeing from creditors and debtors' prison for failed land speculation. He was buried in an obscure country graveyard in Edenton, North Carolina.[33] Today, Wilson is virtually unknown to the American public, even though he was among the most trenchant minds and influential delegates at the Constitutional Convention (making more speeches than any other delegate, save Gouverneur Morris), and he stamped an indelible mark on American legal theory through his influential law lectures and tenure on the U.S. Supreme Court. Robert Morris, a signer of the Declaration of Independence, Articles of Confederation, and Constitution, a member of the first federal Congress, and the indispensable "financier of the Revolution"—a man who by any measure should be remembered as a Founding Father—similarly borrowed heavily and failed miserably in western land speculation. He languished for three and a half years in a debtors' prison (February 1798 to August 1801), and his reputation has never recovered.

Finally, there seems to be an inclination among modern scholars to dismiss, discount, or ignore the views of pious Founders whose ideas and actions were shaped by deeply held religious convictions. Trained in the rationalist traditions of the academy, some scholars are unfamiliar or uncomfortable with or closed to religiously informed arguments and rhetoric; thus, they dismiss as serious thinkers or otherwise decline to engage Founders whose worldview was profoundly religious. Founders steeped in the rationalist traditions of the Enlightenment are more familiar and accessible, and their exploits are advanced in modern scholarship. John Witherspoon's faith-based perspectives may have scared off more than one secular scholar; moreover, his clerical collar may have symbolically entangled church and state too excessively for modern sensibilities. Jeffry H. Morrison has opined that even in his day some citizens were uneasy with the idea of a clergyman-turned-politician, and "present-day Americans have become even more scrupulous about keeping church separate from state."[34] The profiles of Samuel Adams, Roger Sherman, Oliver Ellsworth, John Jay, Elias Boudinot, and Isaac Backus, among others, may have been similarly diminished by modern secular scholars on account of their profoundly religious identities and perspectives.

DOES THE DIFFERENCE MATTER?

Does the distinction in the public mind between famous Founders and forgotten Founders matter to us today? Yes, it matters for both symbolic and substantive reasons. An exclusive or even primary focus on a small fraternity of famous Founders gives a limited and, thus, potentially distorted picture of the Founders—their ideas, values, interests, aspirations, faith commitments, socioeconomic standings, etc. It slights, if not ignores, the services, sacrifices, and legacies of those forgotten Founders who did much to birth a new nation.

Separating the famous from the now forgotten Founders may convey the erroneous notion that the Founders comprised a much more single-minded, monolithic fraternity than they really did. It obscures the Founders' diverse backgrounds, interests, perspectives and, even biases, projecting an incomplete picture of this generation. Our understanding of the delicate balance of personalities, perspectives, and experiences so vital to the success of the Founding generation is obfuscated when we train our sights on a select few famous Founders and disregard the rest. As previously noted, for example, the most orthodox Christians among the Founders (Samuel Adams, Elias Boudinot, Oliver Ellsworth, Patrick Henry, John Jay, Roger Sherman, and John Witherspoon) are rarely counted among the company of famous Founders, despite their substantial contributions to the new nation, suggesting, perhaps, that the Founders (and, more important, their ideas) were more heterodox than they really were. The contributions of traditional Christian thought to the American Founding are, in large measure, diminished in the process. The unfortunate result is that we discount the views of a significant segment of the Founding generation because they were not shared by a select few famous Founders or we erroneously ascribe to an entire generation or a large company of forgotten Founders the views of an elite few. The views of a handful of famous Founders, in short, are not necessarily representative of all the Founders.

These distortions, unfortunately, are sometimes translated into modern law and policy. Judicial interpretations of the First Amendment illustrate the potential problems. The U.S. Supreme Court's near exclusive reliance on the views of Thomas Jefferson

and James Madison, two purported advocates of church-state separation, to divine the original understanding of the First Amendment, while ignoring the input of others who, in the deliberative
process, championed an essential role for religion in public life, has
promulgated an arguably distorted construction of that amendment. Mark David Hall has documented that, in its recourse to
history, the U.S. Supreme Court has given inordinate attention
to Jefferson and Madison.[35] The focus on these two Virginians
is odd, if not counter historical, because Jefferson, at most, was
indirectly involved in framing the First Amendment (he was serving as the American minister to France when the first Congress
framed the amendment), and Madison suffered decisive defeats
in his efforts to shape the content of the religion provisions. As
Cushing Strout observed: "Madison did not carry the country
along with Virginia's sweeping separation of churches from the
state: indeed, the country in some degree carried him."[36] At critical
junctures in the first Congress's deliberations on the amendment,
language was proposed by Samuel Livermore of New Hampshire
and Fisher Ames of Massachusetts that arguably shaped the final
text of the First Amendment. Legislative histories often gloss over
these crucial contributions and insights of the now all but forgotten Livermore and Ames, suggesting instead that the First Amendment flowed fully formed from the pen of famous Founder James
Madison. Lost in these incomplete histories are the possible concerns and intentions behind Livermore's and Ames's revisions that
almost certainly influenced congressional colleagues, thus leaving
their mark on the First Amendment. In short, a reliance on a short
list of famous Founders may lead us to overlook substantial contributions in thought, word, and deed made by a forgotten Founder.

The near exclusive focus on a select few virtually deified famous
Founders impoverishes our understanding of the American Found-

ing. It also departs from the canons of good scholarship. The demands of thorough, honest scholarship require scholars to give attention to the thoughts, words, and deeds of not only a few selected demigods but also an expansive company of men and women who contributed to the Founding of the American Republic.

NOTES

1. The other was Robert Morris of Pennsylvania.

2. John G. Rommel, *Connecticut's Yankee Patriot: Roger Sherman* (Hartford, Connecticut: The American Revolution Bicentennial Commission of Connecticut, 1979), 28.

3. Joseph J. Ellis, for example, adds Abigail Adams and Aaron Burr to the usual six "most prominent political leaders in the early republic." Ellis, *Founding Brothers: The Revolutionary Generation* (New York: Alfred A. Knopf, 2005), 17.

4. See generally Richard D. Brown, "The Founding Fathers of 1776 and 1787: A Collective View," *William and Mary Quarterly* 3rd ser., 33 (1976): 465–80.

5. Jefferson to Roger C. Weightman, June 24, 1826, in *Thomas Jefferson: Writings*, ed. Merrill D. Peterson (New York: The Library of America, 1984), 1517.

6. Ray Raphael, *Founding Myths: Stories That Hide Our Patriotic Past* (New York: New Press, 2004), 127. See Clinton Rossiter, *1787: The Grand Convention* (New York: Macmillan, 1966), 317 (in the early Republic, "it was generally considered a more noble achievement to have been a Signer of 1776 than a Framer of 1787. . . . [T]he men of 1776 had shaken the earth while the men of 1787 had only helped to settle the dust").

7. Jefferson to John Adams, August 30, 1787, in *Thomas Jefferson: Writings*, 909.

8. Merrill D. Peterson, *The Jefferson Image in the American Mind* (New York: Oxford University Press, 1960), 222. See also Stephen F. Knott, *Alexander Hamilton and the Persistence of Myth* (Lawrence: University Press of Kansas, 2002).

9. This battle of interpretations, Joseph Ellis notes, is manifested in the "earliest histories of the period." In *History of the Rise, Progress, and Termination of the American Revolution* (1805), Mercy Otis Warren set forth the "pure republicanism" or Jeffersonian interpretation, whereas John Marshall articulated an alternative version more friendly to the Federalists in his expansive five-volume *The Life of George Washington* (1804–1807). Ellis, *Founding Brothers*, 13–14.

10. David McCullough, *John Adams* (New York: Simon & Schuster, 2001).

11. Washington was the target of vituperative partisan attacks late in his presidency.

12. Robert Green McCloskey, introduction to *The Works of James Wilson*, ed. Robert Green McCloskey, 2 vols. (Cambridge, MA: The Belknap Press of Harvard University Press, 1967), 1:47.

13. See David W. Maxey, "The Translation of James Wilson," *Supreme Court Historical Society 1990 Yearbook* (1990): 29.

14. Ellis, *Founding Brothers*, 212–27.

15. Jefferson to Madison, February 17, 1826, in *Thomas Jefferson: Writings*, 1515.

16. Douglass Adair, "Fame and the Founding Fathers," in *Fame and the Founding Fathers: Essays by Douglass Adair*, ed. Trevor Colbourn (New York: W. W. Norton & Co.; Institute of Early American History and Culture, 1974), 7.

17. James Wilson, *The Works of James Wilson*, 1:405.

18. Publius [Alexander Hamilton], *Federalist Papers*, no. 72. Cf. John Milton, *Lycidas*, lines 70–72 ("*Fame* is the spur that the clear spirit doth raise / (That last infirmity of Noble mind) / To scorn delights, and live laborious dayes"); Samuel Johnson, *The Rambler* #49 (September 4, 1750) ("the love of fame is to be regulated rather than extinguished; and that men should be taught not to be wholly careless about their memory, but to endeavour that they may be remembered chiefly for their virtues, since no other reputation will be able to transmit any pleasure beyond the grave").

19. Publius [Alexander Hamilton], *Federalist Papers*, no. 72.

20. Adair, "Fame and the Founding Fathers," in *Fame and the Founding Fathers*, 7, 11–12, 24.

21. George Washington, Farewell Address, September 19, 1796, in *The Writings of George Washington*, ed. John C. Fitzpatrick, 37 vols. (Washington, DC: Government Printing Office, 1931–1940), 35:238.

22. This theme, along with Madison's alleged suppression of the so-called Pinckney Plan, is developed in Christopher Collier and James Lincoln Collier, *Decision in Philadelphia: The Constitutional Convention of 1787* (New York: Ballantine Books, 1986), 87–101, 109–11. But see Introduction to *Supplement to Max Farrand's The Records of the Federal Convention of 1787*, ed. James H. Hutson (New Haven: Yale University Press, 1987), xx–xxv.

23. The current George Washington papers project, once completed, is projected to contain approximately ninety volumes. The Adams family papers project is expected to include more than a one hundred volumes. The Thomas Jefferson papers project is estimated to consist of seventy-five volumes. Both the James Madison and Benjamin Franklin papers projects are expected to contain approximately fifty volumes each. The papers of Alexander Hamilton, who died before his fiftieth birthday, were published in twenty-seven volumes. An additional five volumes are devoted to Hamilton's law practice.

24. Gordon S. Wood, *Revolutionary Characters: What Made the Founders Different* (New York: Penguin Press, 2006), 246.

25. George Mason, *The Papers of George Mason, 1725–1792*, ed. Robert A. Rutland, 3 vols. (Chapel Hill: University of North Carolina Press, 1970).

26. Kate Mason Rowland, *The Life of George Mason, 1725–1792*, 2 vols. (New York: Cornell University Library, 1892), 1:272.

27. Jeffry H. Morrison, *John Witherspoon and the Founding of the American Republic* (Notre Dame: University of Notre Dame Press, 2005), 14–15. The twenty-first century has witnessed at least two reprint editions of Witherspoon's works.

28. Warren M. Billings, "'That All Men Are Born Equally Free and Independent': Virginians and the Origins of the Bill of Rights," in *The Bill of Rights and the States: The Colonial and Revolutionary Origins of American Liberties*, ed. Patrick T. Conley and John P. Kaminski (Madison, WI: Madison House, 1992), 337.

29. The Jeffersonian Republican and later Jacksonian charges were that the Federalists, especially Hamilton, were essentially aristocratic (elitist, Anglomaine, and even monarchist), autocratic (vesting excessive power in the executive), antidemocratic, antiagrarian (and pro-urban, manufacturing, and banking interests), and supportive of a strong central or national government. The Federalists, for their part, depicted Jefferson and his followers as Jacobins and zealous advocates of states' rights, diffused governmental power, excessive democracy (mob rule), individualism, and church-state separation (and sometimes heterodoxy). They also emphasized the pro-slavery sentiments of many southern agrarian Republicans.

30. Knott, *Alexander Hamilton and the Persistence of Myth*, 47.

31. Peterson, *The Jefferson Image in the American Mind*, 222; see generally ibid., 209–11, 216–26.

32. Adams to Benjamin Rush, November 14, 1812, in *The Spur of Fame: Dialogues of John Adams and Benjamin Rush, 1805–1813*, ed. John A. Schutz and Douglass Adair (San Marino, CA: The Huntington Library, 1966), 252; Theodore Roosevelt, *Gouverneur Morris: The Story of His Life and Work* (Boston and New York: Houghton, Mifflin and Co., 1898), 251.

33. See Maxey, "The Translation of James Wilson," 29–43.

34. Morrison, *John Witherspoon and the Founding of the American Republic*, 18.

35. Mark David Hall, "Jeffersonian Walls and Madisonian Lines: The Supreme Court's Use of History in Religion Clause Cases," *Oregon Law Review* 85 (2006): 563–614.

36. Cushing Strout, *The New Heavens and New Earth: Political Religion in America* (New York: Harper & Row, 1974), 97.

"The pyramid of government—and a republican government may well receive that beautiful and solid form—should be raised to a dignified altitude: but its foundations must, of consequence, be broad and strong, and deep. The authority, the interests, and the affections of the people at large are the only foundation, on which a superstructure, proposed to be at once durable and magnificent, can be rationally erected."

—*James Wilson*, Lectures on Law, *1791*

"Without liberty, law loses its nature and its name, and becomes oppression. Without law, liberty also loses its nature and its name, and becomes licentiousness."

—*James Wilson*, Lectures on Law, *1791*

JAMES WILSON
(1742–1798)

MARK DAVID HALL

James Wilson was a "reluctant revolutionary," but he played a significant role in the American Revolution and was a signer of the Declaration of Independence. He was one of the most important delegates at the federal Constitutional Convention, where he argued consistently for a strong and democratic national government. His early defense of the proposed Constitution and his leadership in the Pennsylvania ratifying convention did much to secure the Constitution's approval. Wilson served as one of the new nation's first Supreme Court justices, and his Lectures on Law *contains some of the period's most profound commentary on the Constitution and American law.*

WILSON WAS BORN IN CARSKERDO, SCOTLAND, IN 1742, THE SON of a lower-middle-class farmer. Dedicated to the ministry at birth, he received a solid classical education that enabled him to win a scholarship to the University of St. Andrews. Wilson studied there for four years before entering the university's divinity school, St.

Mary's, in 1761. He was forced to withdraw in 1762 upon the death of his father and for a few years served as a tutor to support his family. The life of a pedagogue did not suit Wilson, so as soon as his siblings were old enough to support their mother, he immigrated to America in search of greater opportunities. Arriving in Pennsylvania in 1765, Wilson taught Latin and Greek at the College of Philadelphia (now the University of Pennsylvania) for a year before reading law under John Dickinson. He flourished as an attorney and, as the Revolution approached, was drawn into politics.

Historian Christopher Collier proposed that Wilson was a "polemicist the equal of Tom Paine." This may be an exaggeration, but it is indisputable that Wilson achieved national recognition with his essay "Considerations on the Nature and Extent of the Legislative Authority of the British Parliament" (1774). Many Patriots rejected Parliament's claim that it could levy internal taxes on the colonies, but they conceded that it could regulate and/or tax international trade. Wilson's essay was the first to deny publicly the "legislative authority of the British Parliament over the colonies . . . *in every instance.*" He acknowledged that the colonists owed allegiance to the king in exchange for his protection but stipulated that if the monarch withdrew his protection, the colonists were no longer obligated to obey the Crown. Wilson was able to put this theory into practice after he was appointed to the Second Continental Congress. He was, in Terence Ball's words, "a reluctant revolutionary," but he actively participated in the proceedings and eventually cast a critical vote in favor of independence.

"Revolutionary tract writer, member of Constitutional Congress, prominent member of Constitutional Convention, and Federalist, Supreme Court justice, legal theorist."

—Ralph Ketcham

By the late 1770s, Wilson was recognized as one of the finest attorneys in America. In 1779 he was appointed to be France's advocate-general in the United States. He served in this position until 1783, when he resigned because King Louis XVI was unwilling to pay the high fees he required (the king eventually paid him 10,000 livres for his services). In 1782, Pennsylvania asked Wilson to represent the state in a land dispute with Connecticut. The case was argued before a tribunal formed under Article IX of the Articles of Confederation, and Wilson's careful arguments won the day. His legal prominence is illustrated as well by General Washington's willingness to pay him one hundred guineas to accept his nephew Bushrod as a law student. Bushrod, aware that such a fee was well above the going rate, begged his uncle to allow him to study elsewhere. But Washington was convinced of Wilson's ability as a lawyer and insisted on him, although he had to pay the fee with a promissory note. Bushrod was evidently well served by this arrangement, as indicated by his successful legal career and eventual appointment to his mentor's seat on the Supreme Court of the United States.

In his 1785 pamphlet, "Considerations on the Bank of North America," Wilson made the provocative argument that even under the Articles of Confederation, "[t]o many purposes, the United States are to be considered as one undivided, independent nation." Moreover, he proposed that Congress possessed a variety of implied powers, including the power to charter a national bank, and he vigorously defended the necessity of such a bank. Numerous scholars have noted that the essay contains every argument later made by Alexander Hamilton and his allies in support of a national bank under the United States Constitution.

In 1787 the Pennsylvania legislature appointed Wilson to represent the state at the Constitutional Convention. He attended the Convention from start to finish, and he participated in all of the most significant proceedings. Wilson joined with Madison to argue for a powerful national government based immediately upon the authority of the people. He was the most democratic of all delegates, arguing for the direct, popular, and proportional election of representatives, senators, and the president. When his colleagues rejected the direct election of the president—George Mason said "it would be as unnatural to refer the choice of the proper character for chief Magistrate to the people, as it would, to refer a trial of colours to a blind man"—Wilson, according to Carol Berkin, "devised the electoral college," or, in Collier's words, he became the "father of the bastard electoral college."

Wilson believed that the chief executive should be independent of the legislature and that he should have a range of powers that would allow him to act with "vigor and dispatch." He also fought for an independent federal judiciary that would possess the power of judicial review. Indeed, throughout the Convention he was one of the most significant advocates of checks and balances and the separation of powers. Wilson had more faith in the people than most Founders, but he was convinced that concentrated power, even power concentrated in a legislature, would lead to disaster. In his *Lectures on Law*, he wrote that a "single legislature is calculated to unite in it all the pernicious qualities of the different extremes of bad government." Finally, it is

"Mr. Wilson ranks among the foremost in legal and political knowledge . . . no man is more clear, copious, and comprehensive than Mr. Wilson, yet he is no great Orator. He draws attention not by the charm of his eloquence, but by the force of his reasoning."

—William Pierce, Wilson's colleague at the Federal Convention of 1787 important to note that Wilson served on the critical five-member Committee of Detail, and many of the earliest full drafts of the Constitution are in his handwriting.

Under Wilson's leadership, Pennsylvania became the second state, and the first large one, to ratify the Constitution. As the only member of the state's ratifying convention who attended the Federal Convention, Wilson was in an excellent position to defend the Constitution. In his "State House Yard Speech" of October 6, 1787, he responded to the earliest Anti-Federalist criticisms. Gordon S. Wood in *The Creation of the American Republic: 1776–1787* remarked that this speech quickly became "the basis of all Federalist thinking." Wilson did his job so well that Federalists throughout the country enlisted his aid in their states' ratification debates. George Washington, for instance, sent a copy of the speech to a friend, noting:

> the enclosed *Advertiser* contains a speech of Mr. Wilson's, as able, candid, and honest member as was in the convention, which will place most of Colonel Mason's objections in their true point of light, I send it to you. The republication of it, if you can get it done, will be serviceable at this juncture.

By the end of 1787, the speech had been reprinted in thirty-four newspapers in twelve states, and it was circulated in pamphlet form throughout the nation. Bernard Bailyn wrote in *The Ideological Origins of the American Revolution* that "in the 'transient circumstances' of the time it was not so much the *Federalist* papers that captured most people's imaginations as James Wilson's speech of October 6, 1787, the most famous, to some the most notorious, federalist statement of the time." Similarly, political scientist Gordon Lloyd commented that the "State-House speech is vital for an understanding of the pamphlet exchanges during the struggle for ratification." Following the ratification of the U.S. Constitution, Wilson played a major role in the Pennsylvania constitutional convention of 1789–1790.

George Washington appointed Wilson to be associate justice of the United States Supreme Court in 1789. The Court had relatively little business during its first decade, but Wilson issued significant opinions or votes in several cases, including *Hylton v. U.S.* (1796), *Ware v. Hylton* (1796), and *Chisholm v. Georgia* (1793). Particularly important is his seriatim opinion in *Chisholm*. In this case the Court had to determine if Alexander Chisholm, a citizen of South Carolina, could sue the state of Georgia. Georgia claimed he could not because it was a sovereign state. Wilson famously responded that "[a]s to the purposes of the Union . . . Georgia is NOT a sovereign State." He reasoned that by ratifying the Constitution, the citizens of Georgia gave the federal judiciary, in the language of Article III, the power to judge controversies "between a State and Citizens of another State." This ruling provoked an immediate storm of outrage. There was talk of impeachment, and the day after the decision an amendment was introduced in Congress to overturn it. With the ratification of the Eleventh Amendment in 1795, the Court's decision in *Chisholm* was negated, but Wilson's opinion remains an important statement of the basic principles of American federalism.

> *"James Wilson was arguably the best legal theorist of the Founders."*
>
> —Garry Wills

Perhaps the most significant but overlooked case with which Wilson was involved concerned the Invalid Pension Act of 1792. The law required federal judges to act as administrators to determine whether veterans were eligible for certain benefits. In *Hay-*

burn's Case (1792), Wilson, who was riding circuit, led Justice John Blair and District Court judge Richard Peters to declare the act unconstitutional because it required judges to perform nonjudicial duties. Congress rapidly altered the act to meet Wilson's objections, so the Supreme Court never heard the case. Accordingly, *Hayburn's Case* is often overlooked as the first instance where a federal court declared an act of Congress to be unconstitutional.

From 1790 to 1792, Wilson offered a series of law lectures at the College of Philadelphia—today the University of Pennsylvania. Because he believed that law should be "studied and practised as a science founded in principle," not "followed as a trade depending merely upon precedent," many of his lectures are devoted to broad moral, epistemological, political, and jurisprudential issues. Consequently, they contain some of the richest analysis of America's constitutional order written by a Founder. Their significance was recognized by many survey participants. For instance, Garry Wills suggested that "Wilson was arguably the best legal theorist of the Founders." In a similar vein, Howard L. Lubert called Wilson "a leading legal authority of the age," and Walter Nicgorski wrote that he was "a ranging, profound, and bold thinker, both about the principles of good government and about specific constitutional devices," while Henry J. Abraham referred to him as "one of the outstanding lawyer scholars of his time."

In the early 1770s, Wilson began speculating heavily in western land. In 1797 an economic downturn devastated an overleveraged Wilson. Even though he was a sitting Supreme Court justice, he was thrown into jail on two separate occasions because of unpaid debts. He spent his final days hiding from creditors in Edenton, North Carolina. Wilson died on August 21, 1798, and was buried with little ceremony in Edenton. In 1906 his body was disinterred and reburied in America's Westminster Abbey–Christ Church, Philadelphia.

> *"Wilson was second to James Madison in importance in framing the Constitution. Wilson was also the leading American legal theorist of his day."*
>
> —Scott Gerber

Wilson's inglorious and early death, his lack of papers, and his service on the Supreme Court at a time when there was little business before that body conspired to keep him in relative obscurity. He is worthy, however, of serious consideration as one of the most thoughtful and systematic political and legal theorists of the Founding era. He played a critical role at the Constitutional Convention, and although he did not win every battle, the American constitutional system has developed over time to closely resemble his vision. In his law lectures, Wilson wrote:

> There is not in the whole science of politicks a more solid or a more important maxim than this—that of all governments, those are the best, which, by the natural effect of their constitutions, are frequently drawn back to their first principles.

If American citizens, like governments, should reflect upon the first principles of our constitutional republic, the political and legal ideas of one of the greatest theorists among the Founders simply cannot be ignored.

Main Contributions of James Wilson

Wilson played a critical role in drafting the United States Constitution. He consistently argued for a strong and democratic national government that would protect the natural rights of its citizens.

Wilson offered one of the earliest and most influential responses to anti-Federalist criticisms of the Constitution. Under his leadership, Pennsylvania became the second state to ratify the document.

Wilson was one of the leading political and legal theorists among all of the Founders.

From the Pen of James Wilson

O f law there are different kinds. All, however, may be arranged in two different classes. 1. Divine. 2. Human laws. The descriptive epithets employed denote, that the former have God, the latter, man, for their author. The laws of God may be divided into the following species.

I. That law, the book of which we are neither able nor worthy to open. Of this law, the author and observer is God. He is a law to himself, as well as to all created things. This law we may name the "law eternal."

II. That law, which is made for angels and the spirits of the just made perfect. This may be called the "law celestial." This law, and the glorious state for which it is adapted, we see, at present, but darkly and as through a glass: but hereafter we shall see even as we are seen; and shall know even as we are known. From the wisdom and the goodness of the adorable Author and Preserver of the universe, we are justified in concluding, that the celestial and perfect state is governed, as all other things are, by his established laws. What those laws are, it is not yet given us to know; but on one truth we may rely with sure and certain confidence—those laws are wise and good. For another truth we have infallible authority—those laws are strictly obeyed: "In heaven his will is done."

III. That law, by which the irrational and inanimate parts

of the creation are governed. The great Creator of all things has established general and fixed rules, according to which all the phenomena of the material universe are produced and regulated. These rules are usually denominated laws of nature. The science, which has those laws for its object, is distinguished by the name of natural philosophy. It is sometimes called, the philosophy of body. Of this science, there are numerous branches.

IV. That law, which God has made for man in his present state; that law, which is communicated to us by reason and conscience, the divine monitors within us, and by the sacred oracles, the divine monitors without us. This law has undergone several subdivisions, and has been known by distinct appellations, according to the different ways in which it has been promulgated, and the different objects which it respects.

As promulgated by reason and the moral sense, it has been called natural; as promulgated by the holy scriptures, it has been called revealed law.

As addressed to men, it has been denominated the law of nature; as addressed to political societies, it has been denominated the law of nations.

But it should always be remembered, that this law, natural or revealed, made for men or for nations, flows from the same divine source: it is the law of God.

Nature, or, to speak more properly, the Author of nature, has done much for us; but it is his gracious appointment and will, that we should also do much for ourselves. What we do, indeed, must be founded on what he has done; and the deficiencies of our laws must be supplied by the perfections of his. Human law must rest its authority, ultimately, upon the authority of that law, which is divine.

Of that law, the following are maxims—that no injury should be done—that a lawful engagement, voluntarily made, should be faithfully fulfilled. We now see the deep and the solid foundations of human law.

It is of two species. 1. That which a political society makes for itself. This is municipal law. 2. That which two or more political societies make for themselves. This is the voluntary law of nations.

In all these species of law—the law eternal—the law celestial— the law natural—the divine law, as it respects men and nations— the human law, as it also respects men and nations—man is deeply and intimately concerned. Of all these species of law, therefore, the knowledge must be most important to man.

Those parts of natural philosophy, which more immediately relate to the human body, are appropriated to the profession of physick.

The law eternal, the law celestial, and the law divine, as they are disclosed by that revelation, which has brought life and immortality to light, are the more peculiar objects of the profession of divinity.

The law of nature, the law of nations, and the municipal law form the objects of the profession of law.

From this short, but plain and, I hope, just statement of things, we perceive a principle of connexion between all the learned professions; but especially between the two last mentioned. Far from being rivals or enemies, religion and law are twin sisters, friends, and mutual assistants. Indeed, these two sciences run into each other. The divine law, as discovered by reason and the moral sense, forms an essential part of both.

From this statement of things, we also perceive how important and dignified the profession of the law is, when traced to its sources, and viewed in its just extent.

The immediate objects of our attention are, the law of nature, the law of nations, and the municipal law. On the two first of these three great heads, I shall be very general. On the last, especially on those parts of it, which comprehend the constitutions and publick law, I shall be more particular and minute.

—James Wilson, *Lectures on Law* (1791)

Recommended Reading

Kermit L. Hall and Mark David Hall, ed. *Collected Works of James Wilson*, 2 vols. (Indianapolis: Liberty Fund Press, 2007).

Mark David Hall, *The Political and Legal Philosophy of James Wilson, 1742–1798* (Columbia, MO: The University of Missouri Press, 1997).

Charles Page Smith, *James Wilson: Founding Father, 1742–1798* (Chapel Hill: University of North Carolina Press, 1956).

"Every Member of Society is in Duty bound to contribute to the Safety & Good of the Whole; and when the Subject is of such Importance as the Liberty & Happiness of a Country, every inferior Consideration, as well as the Inconvenience to a few Individuals, must give place to it; nor is this any Hardship upon them; as themselves & their Posterity are to partake of the Benefits resulting from it."

—George Mason to Richard Henry Lee, June 7, 1770

"We came equals into this world, and equals shall we go out of it. All men are by nature born equally free and independent. To protect the weaker from the injuries and insults of the stronger were societies first formed. . . . Every society, all government, and every kind of civil compact therefore, is or ought to be, calculated for the general good and safety of the community. Every power, every authority vested in particular men is, or ought to be, ultimately directed to this sole end; and whenever any power or authority whatever extends further, or is of longer duration than is in its nature necessary for these purposes, it may be called government, but it is in fact oppression. . . . In all our associations; in all our agreements let us never lose sight of this fundamental maxim—that all power was originally lodged in, and consequently is derived from, the people. We should wear it as a breastplate, and buckle it on as our armour."

—George Mason, "Remarks on Annual Election for the Fairfax Independent Company," April 1775

"Slavery discourages arts & manufactures. The poor despise labor when performed by slaves. They prevent the immigration of Whites, who really enrich & strengthen a Country. They produce the most pernicious effect on manners. Every master of slaves is born a petty tyrant. They bring the judgment of heaven on a Country. As nations can not be rewarded or punished in the next world they must be in this. By an inevitable chain of causes & effects providence punishes national sins, by national calamities."

—George Mason, Speech in Constitutional Convention, August 22, 1787

GEORGE MASON
(1725–1792)

DANIEL L. DREISBACH

George Mason played pivotal roles in important representative assemblies of his state and nation, including Virginia Conventions in 1775 and 1776, the Constitutional Convention of 1787, and the Virginia ratifying convention in June 1788. His contributions to the political documents of the Founding era are his most enduring legacy. He was the principal draftsman of the Fairfax Resolves, Virginia's first state constitution, and, most famously, Virginia's Declaration of Rights, which is still enshrined in the Commonwealth's laws. The Virginia Declaration influenced numerous state, national, and international declarations of rights and informed essential phrases in the U.S. Declaration of Independence. At the Constitutional Convention of 1787, Mason labored to shape the national constitution, but, in the end, he refused to sign it and led the campaign to thwart its ratification. After unsuccessfully moving to add a bill of rights to the proposed national constitution, he became a leading advocate for such

*a bill, which was eventually added to the U.S. Constitution
in December 1791.*

GEORGE MASON IV (1725–1792) WAS BORN ON HIS FAMILY'S FAIRFAX
County plantation in December 1725. He inherited the estate a
decade later when his father drowned in a boating accident on the
Potomac River. The young Mason received little formal education, although he was tutored at home and read extensively in his
uncle's library, one of the best in colonial Virginia. He married
Ann Eilbeck of Maryland in 1750—a marriage that, before Ann's
death in 1773, produced twelve children, nine of whom survived
to adulthood. During the marriage, Mason built a home he called
Gunston Hall near the Potomac, a few miles south of Mount Vernon. In 1780 he married Sarah Brent who was from a prominent
Maryland family.

In addition to managing a prosperous plantation, Mason
assumed a variety of community offices and responsibilities,
including vestryman and church warden of Truro Parish, justice
of the Fairfax County court, trustee of the city of Alexandria, and
elected member of the House of Burgesses, the Commonwealth's
colonial legislature. In the late 1740s, Mason invested in and later
became an officer of the Ohio
Company, which speculated
in western lands. Represent-
ing the company's disputed
claims was a preoccupation of
his adult life.

*"Author of the Virginia Bill
of Rights who should be better
known as the father of all bills
of rights, especially the U.S.
one of 1791—also for his anti-
slavery efforts in the Convention of 1787."*

—Christopher Collier

Starting in the mid-1760s,
Mason began to articulate the
colonists' claims to liberty and
privileges as Englishmen and

their grievances against the Crown, especially onerous taxes. He drafted the Fairfax Resolves in July 1774, an influential statement expressing the colonists' constitutional rights and objections to British policies in the wake of the Boston Port Act. He also served on the Fairfax County Committee of Safety and the Committee of Correspondence. He was elected to represent Fairfax County at the Virginia Convention, where he was the lead draftsman of the Virginia Declaration of Rights and Constitution of 1776.

He attended the Mount Vernon Conference in March 1785, an important prelude to the Annapolis Convention (to which Mason was an appointed delegate, but he did not attend) the following year and the Constitutional Convention that met in Philadelphia in 1787. Mason was appointed a Virginia representative to the Constitutional Convention. He was one of the most vocal delegates, contributing significantly to the course of debates and the shape of the final document. He failed, however, to carry the Convention on several issues of importance to him and, therefore, declined to sign the proposed Constitution. He returned home and, in the final political campaign of his career, led the losing effort to defeat the Constitution in the Virginia ratifying convention held in Richmond in June 1788. Mason declined an appointment to the U.S. Senate under the new national Constitution and died at Gunston Hall, where he was buried in October 1792.

Today, Mason is best known as the principal draftsman of the Virginia Declaration of Rights, adopted on June 12, 1776. He was a Fairfax County delegate to the Virginia Convention, filling the seat vacated by George Washington, who had been appointed commander in chief of the Continental Army. The Convention of 1776, arguably the most noteworthy political body ever assembled in the Commonwealth's history, convened in Williamsburg on May 6, 1776. On May 15, the convention passed a resolution instructing the commonwealth's delegates at the Continental Congress to press for a declaration of independence from England. This bold initiative raised questions about the nature of civil authority extant in the commonwealth. Believing, perhaps, that they had reverted to a state of nature, the delegates thought it necessary to frame a new social compact, beginning with a declaration of man's natural rights, followed by a new plan of civil government. The assembly appointed a committee to prepare a state declaration of rights and constitution. Among those appointed to the committee were Mason and the young, untested delegate from Orange County, James Madison Jr.

Mason, whose considerable talents were well known in the commonwealth, was a driving force in the convention. Edmund Pendleton informed Thomas Jefferson that "Colo[nel] Mason seems to have the Ascendancy in the great work" of forming a new government in Virginia. Some time in late May, Mason prepared ten proposals for a declaration of rights to which other proposals were added by the committee. Committee drafts of the declaration were printed and circulated widely up and down the Atlantic seaboard in late May and early June, and they had an immediate and profound impact on compatriots in the nascent states engaged in the task of creating new governments. Interestingly, a committee draft, not the version ultimately enacted, had the most influence in the other states.

The Virginia Declaration was printed in draft form, thoroughly debated, and amended before it was passed unanimously on June 12. The genius of Mason's Declaration of Rights was not that it expressed original principles; rather, it distilled and harmonized the republican sentiments of the day, brilliantly summarizing the objectives of those Americans who aspired to be independent and free. With remarkable brevity and clarity, it condensed the great principles of political freedom inherited from the British, including principles extracted from the Magna Carta, the Petition of Right, the English Bill of Rights, and the long struggle to establish parliamentary supremacy culminating in the Glorious Revolution of 1688. It combined a commitment to fundamental liberties with a brief expression of constitutional doctrines and political ideas expounded by Locke, Montesquieu, and other liberal political philosophers.

The Declaration of Rights, which Mason boasted was the "first in America," is acclaimed as a guidepost to the republican principles of the American Founding. By the end of the Founding era, every state had either framed a bill of rights or enacted legislation with similar provisions. Many states, including Pennsylvania, Maryland, North Carolina, Vermont, Delaware, New Hampshire, and Massachusetts, apparently undertook this task with a copy of the Virginia Declaration before them. The national Bill of Rights, ratified in 1791, similarly bears the unmistakable influence of Mason's declaration. Christopher Collier, a scholar of the American Founding, said Mason "should be better known as the father of all bills of rights, especially the U.S. one of 1791."

> *"Nobody understood better (except maybe some Massachusetts townsmen) the meaning of popular sovereignty. He cared about rights. He deserves to be remembered with honor."*
>
> —Pauline Maier

The declaration contains sixteen articles, affirming the "inherent rights" of life, liberty, property, and the pursuit of happiness and safety; describing government power as vested in and derived from the people; outlining the separation of the state's "legislative and executive powers" from the "judiciary"; and enumerating individual rights that are free from government restrictions. The first

article famously declares (in a sentence that informed the open-
ing lines of the U.S. Declaration of Independence) "THAT all
men are by nature equally free and independent, and have certain
inherent rights . . . [that they cannot divest]; namely, the enjoyment of life and liberty, with the means of acquiring and possessing property, and pursuing and obtaining happiness and safety."
Pauline Maier, an eminent historian of the Declaration of Independence, observed that Mason's "phrase 'all men are born equally
free and independent' [as the phrase appeared in Mason's original
draft] influenced the Declaration of Independence and one state's
Declaration of Rights after another. Those are perhaps some of
the most important words in any American Founding document."

Among the enumerated rights it sets forth are those of a criminal defendant to be informed of accusations, "confronted with
the accusers and witnesses, to call for evidence in his favour, and
to a speedy trial by an impartial jury of his vicinage"; the privi-
lege against self-incrimination; the guarantee of due process of
law; prohibitions on "excessive bail," "excessive fines," "cruel and
unusual punishments," and unreasonable searches and seizures;
the "freedom of the press"; and the "free exercise of religion."

After adopting the Declaration of Rights, the convention
turned its attention to framing a constitution or form of government. Once again, Mason was the chief architect. The Virginia
Constitution of June 1776 was one of the first written state constitutions and a model followed by other states. Republican in character, the brief document separated the powers of the "legislative,
executive, and judiciary departments," created a bicameral legislature whose members were elected by the people, placed term limits on key government offices, provided that government officials
could be impeached for "mal-administration [or] corruption," and
directed the legislature to elect the governor and appoint judges.

One significant defect was that it failed to provide for an amending process. The state constitution reflected the view, expressed in the Declaration of Rights, that the people are the source of all legitimate governmental power.

In December 1786, Virginia appointed Mason as one of its delegates to an assembly convened in Philadelphia to revise the Articles of Confederation. He agreed to serve. At the Constitutional Convention, he spoke more frequently than all but four delegates. His contributions confirmed that he was an astute student of law, politics, and constitutionalism.

He advocated popular elections, liberal suffrage requirements, the initiation of money bills in the House of Representatives, a three-person executive, a limited role for the federal judiciary, the admission of and full equality for new states in the west, and a termination of the importation of slaves. Although he depended on and profited from slave labor and declined in his lifetime or in his will to free his own slaves, he made several statements in the Convention against the peculiar institution and, more specifically, slave importation. "Slavery discourages arts & manufactures," he said in one speech. "They produce the most pernicious effect on manners. Every master of slaves is born a petty tyrant. They bring the judgment of heaven on a Country." Most famously, he championed a national declaration of rights. In the Convention's closing days, he spearheaded an effort to draw up a bill of rights. The state delegations unanimously rejected this initiative. The absence of support for Mason's proposal did not indicate hostility to the concept of rights. Rather, there was a consensus that the national government under the proposed Constitution had no jurisdiction in matters pertaining to civil and religious liberties; and where no power had been granted, there was no need to check the abuse of power.

When the Convention failed to address his objections to the emerging national charter, especially the absence of a declaration of rights and the power given Congress to enact navigation laws by a simple majority vote, Mason exclaimed "that he would sooner chop off his right hand than put it to the Constitution as it now stands." Much to the consternation of the Constitution's supporters, Mason refused to sign the document. "Col. Mason left Philad[elphi]a in an exceeding ill humour indeed," James Madison reported. "He considers the want of a Bill of Rights as a fatal objection."

Before departing from Philadelphia in September 1787, Mason drafted a statement outlining his objections to the proposed Constitution. It was published shortly thereafter and widely circulated, framing the debate over the Constitution's ratification. As an incisive critic and active opponent of the proposed Constitution, Mason (along with other articulate Anti-Federalists) defined and drove the debate on certain constitutional issues and features, especially the need for a national bill of rights. Many of the trenchant defenses of the Constitution were direct responses to Anti-Federalist critiques, such as Mason's.

> *"His thinking about rights is important to engage."*
>
> —Walter Nicgorski

Back in Virginia, Mason was elected to the state's ratifying convention, where, in concert with Patrick Henry and William Grayson, he led the opposition to the proposed Constitution. "No Bill of Rights" became the rallying slogan of Mason and the Anti-Federalists. The campaign in Virginia to derail ratification lost narrowly.

While the first federal Congress was still debating amendments, Mason wrote: "I have received much Satisfaction from the

Amendments to the federal Constitution, which have lately passed the House of Representatives; I hope they will also pass the Senate. With two or three further Amendments . . . I cou'd chearfully put my Hand & Heart to the new Government." The amendments Mason had in mind were so substantial and sweeping that the measures actually adopted almost certainly did not assuage his concerns. Nonetheless, he obtained a measure of satisfaction with the ratification of the national Bill of Rights in December 1791.

What explains Mason's relative obscurity today? The irascible, independent-minded Mason was a most reluctant public figure. He eschewed the spotlight, preferring to attend to the pressing demands of his family and plantation. He lacked the diplomatic skills, penchant for self-promotion, and gifts of soaring oratory that might have brought him more acclaim. His precarious health (a chronic affliction with gout for most of his adult life substantially interfered with public duties), truculent temperament, and aversion to political life all contributed to a diminished profile in the history of the Founding era. He declined an office in the national government under the ratified Constitution (refusing an appointment to the U.S. Senate) and died in 1792 at a time when more-famous Founders were assuming leading roles on the newly available national stage. His outspoken opposition to the Constitution, more than anything, diminished his reputation as a Founder. Moreover, unlike the famous Founders, he died leaving relatively few papers and no memoirs documenting his salient contributions to his state and nation.

Although Mason is an almost forgotten Founder, he was recognized by his contemporaries as, in the words of Thomas Jefferson, "one of our really great men, and of the first order of greatness." In his *Autobiography*, Jefferson described Mason as a formidable debater, "one most steadfast, able and zealous. . . . This was George

Mason, a man of the first order of wisdom among those who acted on the theatre of the revolution, of expansive mind, profound judgment, cogent in argument, learned in the lore of our former constitution, and earnest for the republican change on democratic principles." William Pierce, a Georgia delegate at the Constitutional Convention, said Mason was "a Gentleman of remarkable strong powers, and possesses a clear and copious understanding. He is able and convincing in debate, steady and firm in his principles, and undoubtedly one of the best politicians in America." James Madison thought that Mason possessed "the high character of a powerful Reasoner, a profound Statesman and a devoted Republican."

Significantly, Mason's contemporaries lamented that he had not been accorded the recognition and honor due to him. Philip Mazzei, the Italian physician, merchant, and admirer of American liberty, remarked: "[I]in my opinion . . . he is not well enough known. He is one of those brave, rare-talented men who cause Nature a great effort to produce,—a Dante, a Macchiavelli, a Galileo, a Newton, a Franklin, a Turgot, an Elvezio, and so on." Madison opined, "It is to be regretted that, highly distinguished as he was, the memorials of them we record, or perhaps otherwise attainable, are more scanty than of many of his contemporaries far inferior to him in intellectual powers and in public services."

Mason received a small, albeit belated, measure of recognition for his monumental contributions to his state and nation when, in April 2002, the National Park Service dedicated a modest George Mason Memorial in a secluded corner of the National Mall in Washington, D.C.

MAIN CONTRIBUTIONS OF GEORGE MASON

Mason was the author of the Fairfax Resolves in July 1774, which articulated the colonists' constitutional claims against the British.

He was a delegate to the Virginia Convention of 1776, where he was the principal draftsman of the commonwealth's influential declaration of rights, adopted June 12, 1776, and first constitution following independence, adopted June 29, 1776. Both documents were models used by other states.

He was a Virginia delegate to and one of the most valuable members of the Constitutional Convention of 1787. He became a leading critic of the proposed U.S. Constitution, in part because it lacked a bill of rights, and led a campaign to defeat its ratification.

From the Pen
of George Mason

A DECLARATION *of* RIGHTS *made by the representatives of the good people of Virginia, assembled in full and free Convention; which rights do pertain to them, and their posterity, as the basis and foundation of government.*

1. THAT all men are by nature equally free and independent, and have certain inherent rights, of which, when they enter into a state of society, they cannot, by any compact, deprive or divest their posterity; namely, the enjoyment of life and liberty, with the means of acquiring and possessing property, and pursuing and obtaining happiness and safety.

2. That all power is vested in, and consequently derived from, the people; that magistrates are their trustees and servants, and at all time amenable to them.

3. That government is, or ought to be, instituted for the common benefit, protection, and security, of the people, nation, or community, of all the various modes and forms of government that is best, which is capable of producing the greatest degree of happiness and safety, and is most effectually secured against the danger of mal-administration; and that whenever any government shall be found inadequate or contrary to these purposes, a majority of the community hath an indubitable, unalienable, and indefea-

sible right, to reform, alter, or abolish it, in such manner as shall be judged conducive to the publick weal.

4. That no man, or set of men, are entitled to exclusive or separate emoluments or privileges from the community, but in consideration of publick services; which, not being descendible, neither ought the offices of magistrate, legislator, or judge, to be hereditary.

5. That the legislative and executive powers of the state should be separate and distinct from the judiciary; and that the members of the two first may be restrained from oppression, by feeling and participating the burthens of the people, they should, at fixed periods, be reduced to a private station, return into that body from which they were originally taken, and the vacancies be supplied by frequent, certain, and regular elections, in which all, or any part of the former members, to be again eligible, or ineligible, as the laws shall direct.

6. That elections of members to serve as representatives of the people, in assembly, ought to be free; and that all men, having sufficient evidence of permanent common interest with, and attachment to, the community, have the right of suffrage, and cannot be taxed or deprived of their property for publick uses without their own consent, or that of their representatives so elected, nor bound by any law to which they have not, in like manner, assented, for the publick good.

7. That all power of suspending laws, or the execution of laws, by any authority without consent of the representatives of the people, is injurious to their rights, and ought not to be exercised.

8. That in all capital or criminal prosecutions a man hath a right to demand the cause and nature of his accusation, to be confronted with the accusers and witnesses, to call for evidence in his favour, and to a speedy trial by an impartial jury of his vicinage,

without whose unanimous consent he cannot be found guilty, nor can he be compelled to give evidence against himself; that no man be deprived of his liberty except by the law of the land, or the judgment of his peers.

9. That excessive bail ought not to be required, nor excessive fines imposed, nor cruel and unusual punishments inflicted.

10. That general warrants, whereby any officer or messenger may be commanded to search suspected places without evidence of a fact committed, or to seize any person or persons not named, or whose offence is not particularly described and supported by evidence, are grievous and oppressive, and ought not to be granted.

11. That in controversies respecting property, and in suits between man and man, the ancient trial by jury is preferable to any other, and ought to be held sacred.

12. That the freedom of the press is one of the great bulwarks of liberty, and can never be restrained but by despotick governments.

13. That a well regulated militia, composed of the body of the people, trained to arms, is the proper, natural, and safe defence of a free state; that standing armies, in time of peace, should be avoided, as dangerous to liberty: and that, in all cases, the military should be under strict subordination to, and governed by, the civil power.

14. That the people have a right to uniform government; and therefore, that no government separate from, or independent of, the government of Virginia, ought to be erected or established within the limits thereof.

15. That no free government, or the blessing of liberty, can be preserved to any people but by a firm adherence to justice, moderation, temperance, frugality, and virtue, and by frequent recurrence to fundamental principles.

16. That religion, or the duty which we owe to our CREATOR, and the manner of discharging it, can be directed only by reason and conviction, not by force or violence, and therefore all men are equally entitled to the free exercise of religion, according to the dictates of conscience; and that it is the mutual duty of all to practice Christian forbearance, love, and charity, towards each other.

—George Mason, Virginia Declaration of Rights (June 12, 1776)

Recommended Reading

Jeff Broadwater, *George Mason: Forgotten Founder* (Chapel Hill: University of North Carolina Press, 2006).

Helen Hill Miller, *George Mason: Gentleman Revolutionary* (Chapel Hill: University of North Carolina Press, 1975).

Kate Mason Rowland, *The Life of George Mason, 1725–1792,* 2 vols. (New York: G. P. Putnam's Sons, 1892).

Robert A. Rutland, *George Mason: Reluctant Statesman* (Baton Rouge: Louisiana State University Press, 1961).

"In adopting a republican form of government, I not only took it as a man does his wife, for better or for worse, but what few men do with their wives, I took it knowing all its bad qualities. Neither ingratitude, therefore, nor slander can disappoint expectation nor excite surprise. If, in arduous circumstances, the voice of my country should call for my services, and I have the well-founded belief, that they can be useful, they shall certainly be rendered; but I hope that no such circumstances will arise, and in the mean time, 'pleas'd let me trifle life away.'"

—*Gouverneur Morris to John Dickinson, May 23, 1803*

"It is not easy to be wise for all times, not even for the present— much less for the future; and those who judge of the past must recollect that, when it was present, the present was future."

—*Gouverneur Morris to Robert Walsh, February 5, 1811*

GOUVERNEUR MORRIS
(1752–1816)

JOHN K. BUSH

Gouverneur Morris helped draft the New York Constitution of 1777, and according to James Madison, "the finish given to the style and arrangement of the [U.S.] constitution fairly belongs to the pen of Mr. Morris." He served briefly in the Continental Congress, but in his short tenure he played a critical role in supplying the Continental Army at Valley Forge and signed the Articles of Confederation. From 1781 through 1784, Morris was the assistant superintendent of finance for the Continental Congress. President George Washington appointed him as America's first official secret agent overseas (1788) and the U.S. minister to France (1792–1794). He also served as a U.S. senator from New York from 1800 to 1803. After having many love interests, Morris was the last Founder to marry.

ON JANUARY 31, 1752, GOUVERNEUR MORRIS WAS BORN INTO A prominent New York family at their manorial estate, Morrisania, which is now part of the Bronx in New York City. He graduated from King's College (today Columbia University) at the age of sixteen and afterward apprenticed to be a lawyer. Morris recorded that he tried to model himself "after some persons who cut a figure in the law." He had an "irrepressible tendency to be flippant when he should be serious," as one biographer put it. But a sharp tongue did not impede his many successful business ventures.

When the War for Independence erupted, Morris's family split sharply. He joined with his half brother, Lewis, who signed the Declaration of Independence. Morris wrote his Loyalist mother across enemy lines that he must be "called a rebel" for "sentiments . . . not fashionable among the folks you see." In February 1776 a New York regiment rejected Morris's application to serve as a colonel, probably because his right arm was withered—the result of a scalding from an accident in his youth. Morris apparently lost the commission to a person of lower social rank. He complained to his brother that "a herd of mechanics are preferred before the best families in the colony" but rationalized that "my little abilities [are] more adapted to the deliberations of the cabinet than the glorious labors of the field."

Morris's assessment proved correct. By the age of twenty-five he was serving in New York's Fourth Provincial Congress, which adopted the New York Constitution of 1777. He made a motion to urge future legislatures to abolish slavery and argued that "[t]he rights of human nature and our holy religion loudly call upon us to dispense the blessings of freedom to all mankind." Unfortunately, the motion failed, but it furthered a movement that eventually would lead to abolition in New York.

> *"Morris should be remembered for his antislavery expressions in the Convention of 1787 and many other contributions to the final product of that convention."*
>
> —Christopher Collier

In January 1778, Morris took his seat as one of New York's delegates to the Continental Congress. He served on a committee that traveled to Valley Forge and procured supplies for the Continental forces under General George Washington. Morris literally begged provisions for them, as in a letter written to New York governor George Clinton, which described "the American army, in the heart of America . . . on the point of deserting, having nothing to eat." Morris referred to the days of war as "the seed time of glory as of freedom" and became one of Washington's closest friends. Morris wrote that he was "an advocate for the army" who "loved them from acquaintance with some individuals and for the sufferings which as a body they had bravely and patiently endured."

In the spring of 1780, Morris's left leg was amputated after a runaway carriage accident, and he used a peg leg for the rest of his life. A day after the surgery, a friend tried to cheer him up with musings about good things Providence must have in mind for one who loses a limb. Morris responded, "My good sir, you argue the matter so handsomely and point out the advantages of being without legs, that I am almost tempted to part with the other."

Morris quipped about anything and anyone—not a good trait for a politician. Another delegate wrote that he was "like the elephant in war" who is "more destructive to his friends than to his antagonists." Not surprisingly, he lost his bid for reelection to the Continental Congress. From 1781 through 1784 he was the assistant superintendent of finance, serving as the "right-hand man" to the "Financier" of the Revolution, Robert Morris (no relation).

After the War for Independence, the ensuing struggle for "a more perfect Union"—a phrase Morris would later add to the Constitution's preamble—again called Gouverneur Morris into public service. In the Continental Congress, he had signed the Articles of Confederation, which governed the country when, as

Morris observed, "[t]he state of America was suspended by a hair." He understood the importance of a stronger central government for the new republic to survive and accordingly agreed to serve as one of Pennsylvania's delegates at the Constitutional Convention of 1787.

Morris liked to talk—a "brilliant talker," the historian Henry Adams would emphasize, "whose oratory was apt to verge on the domain of melodrama." In the Constitutional Convention, he made 173 speeches, more than any other delegate, and earned the nickname "the eternal speaker." An admirer wrote that Morris's "language" was "eloquent" and "animated," but a detractor described him as "fickle and inconstant—never pursuing one train of thinking—nor ever regular."

Contemporary scholars are less critical of Morris's verbosity. Daniel L. Dreisbach calls him "one of the most influential" delegates who "made monumental contributions to the final document." For example, Morris, along with James Wilson, promoted "a strong chief executive within the necessary limits demanded by a republican form of government," as Christopher Wolf observes.

Morris also is noted for what he opposed at the Constitutional Convention. He called slavery a "nefarious institution" and "the curse of heaven on the states where it prevailed." He unsuccessfully tried to defeat a constitutional provision that would be eliminated after the Civil War, which counted each slave as three-fifths of a person in calculating a state's population for representation in the House of Representatives and the Electoral College.

Notwithstanding that he lost on slavery issues, Morris was "[o]ne of three who dominated debate," Carol Berkin writes. Scott Gerber concurs that "Morris is probably third in importance in framing the Constitution." Indeed, as chief editor of the document, Morris's contributions were no mere window dressing.

For example, he began the Preamble with the words "We the people" rather than "We the states," a choice that emphasized that the Constitution was a compact between each citizen as opposed to the states. "Those three words may be his

> *"The language of the U.S. Constitution would be much poorer if it were not for the words of Gouverneur Morris."*
>
> —Ryan J. Barilleaux

greatest legacy," his biographer Richard Brookhiser concludes. James Madison wrote: "The finish given to the style and arrangement of the constitution fairly belongs to the pen of Mr. Morris. A better choice could not have been made, as the performance of the task proved. The talents and taste of the author were stamped on the face of it."

Curiously, for the man who was called "the foremost publicist of the Continental Congress," Morris was reluctant to expound in writing on the Constitutional Convention. During the debate, he wrote, "my mind was too much occupied with the interests of our country to keep notes of what we had done." In 1788, Morris declined Alexander Hamilton's request for Morris to help write the essays that would become the *Federalist Papers*. He would later claim, "It is not possible for me to recollect with precision all that passed in the Convention while we were framing the Constitution, and, if I could, it is most probable that meaning may have been conceived from incidental expressions different from that which they were intended to convey, and very different from the fixed opinions of the speaker."

Though he could turn a phrase better than most, Morris preferred action to words. He was soon off to Europe, where he conducted a secret mission in London on behalf of President Washington. He also tried, but failed, to organize a group of international investors to purchase all of the American war debt owed to France. He speculated heavily in securities and land in Europe and America. His "breathtakingly brassy" business dealings, combined with his polarizing personality, made him a controversial person for President Washington to appoint as U.S. minister to France in 1792. He was barely confirmed by the U.S. Senate. Washington explained to Morris:

> Whilst your abilities, knowledge in the affairs of this country, and disposition to serve it were adduced, asserted on one hand, you were charged on the other hand, with levity, and imprudence of conversation and conduct. It was urged, that your habit of expression, indicated a hauteur disgusting to those who happen to differ from you in sentiment; . . . [T]he promptitude with which your brilliant, and lively imagination is displayed, allows too little time for deliberation, and correction; and is the primary cause of those sallies which too often offend, and of that ridicule of characters which begets enmity not easy to be forgotten, but which might easily be avoided if it was under the control of more caution and prudence.

Washington nonetheless expressed confidence that Morris would bring more prudence to bear in his conduct.

But Washington knew from personal experience that Morris was unpredictable. Hamilton had once promised Morris the finest dinner for a dozen friends if he would greet the ever formal Washington with a slap on the back. Supposedly Morris clapped his hand on Washington's shoulder and exclaimed, "My dear general, how happy I am to see you look so well." Washington immediately removed Morris's hand, stepped back, and gave him the coldest stare. "Oh, that look!" Morris later recalled. "The majesty of the

American people was before me. How I wished the floor would open and swallow me!"

As U.S. minister to France, Morris advised King Louis XVI on how to deal with revolutionaries. He later stored some of the monarch's treasure in his desk for safekeeping and aided the royal family in one of their ill-fated attempts to escape the country. Morris also hid in his home French aristocrats who were targeted for execution. He kept a diary and wrote many letters that are among the best primary sources for understanding the French Revolution.

Legend has it that Morris's peg leg saved his life on one occasion in Paris. A mob halted his carriage and was about to drag him out and maul him. "An aristocrat!" they exclaimed in their native language. Morris then supposedly shouted in accented French while brandishing his wooden appendage: "An aristocrat! Yes, truly, who lost his leg in the cause of American liberty!" That silenced the crowd.

To his credit, Morris remained at his diplomatic post well after most ambassadors had fled the terror of Paris. Many American leaders faulted him for being too friendly with the royal family and the aristocratic elements of France, but in retrospect many of his observations regarding the excesses of the French Revolution proved accurate. He correctly predicted the rise of Napoleon Bonaparte and the threat to peace posed by the expansionist French Empire. Morris helped implement Washington's policy of strict neutrality between England and France when many sought to tilt the balance of America's allegiance toward the latter.

After being recalled as ambassador for refusing to fully embrace the French revolutionary government, Morris took a long vacation, touring the Continent from 1795 through 1798. In 1799 he returned to America, where he rebuilt his family's Morrisania estate and resumed his legal practice. From 1800 to 1803, he served as a U.S.

senator from New York. He was not reelected, but he refused to retire. In 1804 he helped found the New York Historical Society; in 1807 he served on a commission that planned the street grid for New York City; and in 1811 he was one of three commissioners who proposed the Erie Canal.

At the age of fifty-seven, Morris also undertook a new venture of a very personal sort—he married Anne Cary Randolph. He had had many love interests through the years, and many people were surprised when he became the last Founder to marry. Some relatives disapproved of his spouse. He replied to one such critic that "if the world were to live with my wife, I should certainly have consulted its taste; but as that happens not to be the case, I thought I might, without offending others, endeavor to suit myself." Mr. and Mrs. Morris had a son, Gouverneur Morris II, who would become a railroad magnate.

> *"One of three who dominated debate at the Constitutional Convention."*
>
> —Carol Berkin

Morris was a staunch Federalist and a fierce opponent of Presidents Thomas Jefferson and James Madison. He wrote that he and Jefferson "differ in our system of politics" and remarked that Jefferson was "cold as a frog." Morris minced no words as to Madison either, stating that he was "unfit for the station of President." He believed a report he heard that "Mr. Jefferson and Mr. Madison . . . are determined on going to war with England as soon as they can bring public opinion up to that measure." Like other Federalists, he was critical of "Mr. Madison's War"—i.e., the War of 1812. Many Federalists took their antiwar stance to an extreme, calling a meeting in Hartford, Connecticut, to plan secession of the northeastern states from the Union. Morris sympathized with the secessionists for a period, but he eventually concluded that their divisive objective was wrong.

By the time of his death in 1816, Morris again supported union of the states and expressed renewed faith in the Constitution. He also lost much of his partisan fervor. A few months before he passed away, Morris told a gathering of Federalists not to be so antagonistic toward the Democratic Republicans, stating, "But, gentlemen, let us forget party, and think of our country. That country embraces both parties. We must endeavor, therefore, to save and benefit both."

Main Contributions of Gouverneur Morris

Morris helped arrange supplies for the Continental Army and maintained the finances of the Continental Congress in the American Revolution.

A man who could turn a phrase, Morris spoke more than any other delegate at the Constitutional Convention and gave speeches remembered for both what they achieved (strong power for the executive branch) and what they did not (abolition of slavery). He was the chief editor of the U.S. Constitution.

Morris served as U.S. minister to France during the French Revolution.

From the Pen of Gouverneur Morris

We the People of the United States in order to form a more perfect Union, establish Justice, insure domestic Tranquility, provide for the common defence, promote the general Welfare, and secure the Blessings of Liberty to ourselves and our Posterity, do ordain and establish this Constitution of the United States of America.

—Preamble to the U.S. Constitution

Recommended Reading

Melanie Randolph Miller, *An Incautious Man: The Life of Gouverneur Morris* (Wilmington, DE: ISI Books, 2008).

Richard Brookhiser, *Gentleman Revolutionary: Gouverneur Morris—The Rake Who Wrote the Constitution* (New York: Free Press, 2003).

William Howard Adams, *Gouverneur Morris: An Independent Life* (New Haven: Yale University Press, 2003).

James J. Kirschke, *Gouverneur Morris: Author, Statesman, and Man of the World* (New York: Thomas Dunne Books, 2005).

"To me it appears important that the American government be preserved as it is, until mature experience shall very plainly point out very useful amendments to our constitution; that we steadily repel all foreign influence and interference, and with good faith and liberality treat all nations as friends in peace, and as enemies in war; neither meddling with their affairs, nor permitting them to meddle with ours. These are the primary objects of my policy. The secondary ones are more numerous, such as, to be always prepared for war, to cultivate peace, to promote religion, industry, tranquility, and useful knowledge, and to secure to all the quiet enjoyment of their rights, by wise and equal laws irresistibly executed. I do not expect that mankind will, before the millennium, be what they ought to be; and therefore, in my opinion, every political theory which does not regard them as being what they are, will probably prove delusive."

—John Jay to Benjamin Vaughan, August 31, 1797

"Liberty and reformation may run mad, and madness of any kind is no blessing. I nevertheless think, that there may be a time for reformation, and a time for change, as well as for other things; all that I contend for is, that they be done soberly, by sober and discreet men, and in due manner, measure, and proportion. It may be said, that this cannot always be the case. It is true, and we can only regret it. We must take men and things as they are, and act accordingly; that is, circumspectly."

—John Jay to William Vaughan, May 26, 1797

JOHN JAY
(1745–1829)

JONATHAN DEN HARTOG

John Jay was a significant actor in the American Founding, serving in many roles and offices. During the Revolution he worked in New York government and was a delegate to both the First and Second Continental Congresses. In 1779, Congress sent him to Europe as minister to Spain and later appointed him to be one of the three American commissioners who negotiated the Peace of Paris, which ended the war. He wrote persuasively and acted effectively to secure the ratification of the Constitution. Under the new government, he became the first chief justice of the United States. When war with England threatened in the 1790s, President Washington sent Jay to negotiate with England, and the end result—the Jay Treaty—helped keep the peace. After serving as New York's governor, Jay retired from public life in 1801. His thirty years of service had done much to help the new nation come into existence and become a stable republic.

JAY WAS A RELUCTANT REVOLUTIONARY. HIS BACKGROUND, TEMPERA-
ment, and legal training all inclined against siding with the Patriot
cause, but that was exactly what Jay did. Born in 1745, Jay was raised
in a family with a strong Huguenot (French Protestant) ancestry, yet
one that was also eager to take on English traits and find a place in
the commercial realm of colonial New York. After graduating from
King's College (today Columbia University), he studied law and was
admitted to the New York bar in 1768. In 1774 he married Sarah
Livingston, daughter of the prominent political leader William Livingston. As the conflict with Great Britain escalated, John became
more involved in public meetings, and New York sent him as a delegate to the First Continental Congress at the age of twenty-nine.

In the Continental Congress, Jay advocated a policy of cautious
yet firm resistance to Great Britain. John Adams found him "a Man
of Wit, well-informed, a good Speaker, and an elegant writer." Jay
drafted the Congress's "Address to the People of Great Britain," a
conciliatory piece that invited Britain to rethink its American policies. Even after military conflict broke out at Lexington and Concord in April 1775, Jay continued to hope for reconciliation. In the
Second Continental Congress, he worked with John Dickinson to
draft the Olive Branch Petition to George III—a last attempt at
compromise that the king refused even to receive.

Recalled to New York, Jay filled a number of state offices. He had
given up hope for peace, believing that "our country was prompted
and impelled to independence by necessity and not by choice," and
so he directed the state's endorsement of the Declaration of Independence. Jay next helped draft the state's first constitution. At the
same time, he wrote "An Address of the Convention of the Representatives of the State of New-York, to Their Constituents," which
encouraged New Yorkers to continue fighting, even as the war
seemed to be going against the Patriots. He also had some responsi-

bility for the organization of New York's militias and even oversaw some spies behind British lines. When New York State established its judicial system, Jay was named its first chief justice. Throughout his life, he believed that established law was necessary for order and good government and sought to advance the rule of law.

In winter 1778 the New York legislature sent Jay back to Congress, and he was soon elected its president. In that role, he had responsibilities for correspondence with foreign nations, and those experiences prepared Jay for his commission as ambassador to Spain. Congress hoped that he could either form an alliance with Spain or at least gain additional loans to support the war effort. Jay approached the assignment pessimistically, and he was not disappointed, since the Spanish court virtually ignored him. He was relieved when Congress sent him to Paris to assist John Adams and Benjamin Franklin in negotiating the terms of the peace treaty with the British. Jay and Adams collaborated closely

> *"Given the astonishing range of his accomplishments—president of the Continental Congress, minister to France and Spain, co-author of the Federalist Papers, first chief justice of the United States, governor of New York, leader of the Federalist Party, early opponent of slavery—it is amazing that Jay is so little known. He deserves better."*
>
> —Wilfred McClay

in the talks with both Great Britain and America's ally France. They decided to go against the wishes of Charles Gravier, the comte de Vergennes, the French foreign minister, and sought a separate peace with Great Britain. Their determined, canny diplomacy gained the United States the best possible terms and laid the groundwork for later westward expansion.

After he returned to the United States in 1784, Jay found that he had been elected once again to Congress. Congress appointed him as its secretary of foreign affairs, which made him responsible for all of the Confederation's diplomatic matters. He bemoaned the way he often had to act from a position of weakness rather than strength. In a series of letters to George Washington, John Adams, and Thomas Jefferson, Jay delineated the failures of the Articles of Confederation and the need for constitutional reforms. Notably, he advocated the creation of an independent chief executive and judiciary and a system of checks and balances. Jay thus welcomed the eventual calling of the Constitutional Convention.

New York chose to send only a small delegation to Philadelphia in 1787, leaving Jay out of the Convention, but he was nevertheless pleased with the proposed Constitution. He fought for the document's ratification in New York, most significantly by joining with Alexander Hamilton and James Madison to write the *Federalist Papers*. He was responsible for *Federalist* numbers 2, 3, 4, 5, and 64, which present a hopeful argument for the adoption of the Constitution. He contended that it would secure preexisting American unity and lay the groundwork for further national success. Jay also wrote the very important "An Address to the People of the State of New-York, on the Subject of the Constitution." This single pamphlet helped sway opinion in New York, which was in a critical position for determining the direction of the nation, and it was republished throughout the country. John Adams recognized that Jay's effort in support of the Constitution was "of more importance than any of the rest, indeed of almost as much weight as all the rest." More recently, the scholar Robert Ferguson observed in his 2004 book, *Reading the Early Republic*, that "the ambiance of [Jay's] writings managed to capture and then hold the imagination of the age."

Jay was also a central figure in the New York ratifying convention. His strategizing and rhetoric took a convention that began opposed to the Constitution and actually moved the delegates to approve it. A sympathetic observer of the scene wrote, "Mr. [Jay]'s reasoning is weighty as gold, polished as silver, and strong as steel." Without Jay's skill and hard work, New York may not have ratified the Constitution, and the new government may never have come into existence.

With the new government formed, President-elect Washington offered Jay his choice of offices, and Jay requested the chief justiceship of the Supreme Court. Washington approved, commenting that Jay possessed the "talents, knowledge, and integrity which are so necessary" for the office. Jay wanted this position because he continued to believe that a solid legal order was essential for the healthy functioning of a republican government. As chief justice, Jay was responsible for overseeing the lower federal courts, annually riding circuit (in New England, then later in the southern states), addressing grand juries, and hearing cases that rose to the Supreme Court. In his jurisprudence, Jay worked to shape national law and policy, as well as to support the nation against foreign powers.

In the 1790s the United States had to confront problems originating from Europe. The French Revolution had begun in 1789 and soon produced international conflict. With France and Great Britain locked in war, America struggled to maintain its neutrality. Conflicts with Great Britain over neutral sailing rights, access to Caribbean ports, remaining British forts in the Northwest Territory, and British encouragement of Indian attacks threatened to drag America into war. To avert such a calamity, President Washington sent Jay as a special emissary to Britain in 1794. Jay negotiated a treaty that, although it did not gain everything

Americans had hoped for, was probably the best that could have been obtained under the circumstances. Returning home, Jay was subjected to considerable abuse by the treaty's critics. After much political wrangling and the determined efforts of President Washington and his allies, however, the Senate approved the treaty. Jay had succeeded in keeping the nation out of war and buying the young republic additional years of peace in which to mature. His reputation, however, suffered under the intense criticism.

In 1795, New York elected Jay as governor, so he resigned his seat on the Supreme Court to serve the next six years in that post. He largely dealt with local matters, such as controlling a yellow fever outbreak and making sure that harbor defenses were in place. Jay's actions also overlapped with increasing national excitement, and in the fever for war with France in 1798, he called up the New York militia. Jay's other accomplishment as governor was to pass a gradual emancipation bill, which eventually ended slavery in New York. After almost thirty years of uninterrupted service, Jay retired from public life in 1801.

> *"Because of his extensive diplomatic service to the new nation, his lead role as an author of the New York Constitution of 1777, his writings during the ratification controversy of 1787–1788 and his instrumental role in New York's vote to ratify the Constitution, and finally his faithful service as the nation's first chief justice in the neglected pre-Marshall period of the Supreme Court's history, Jay deserves recognition as one of the most valuable and constructive members of the group we call the Founding Fathers."*
>
> —R. B. Bernstein

During his career, Jay's principles were clearly republican and Federalist. He strongly supported the American experiment of republican self-government under law, as opposed to the monarchies that then filled Europe. Jay was also a Federalist, not only a supporter of the Constitution but also a member of the Federalist political party that flourished in the 1790s and into the 1800s. As his correspondence and speeches indicate, Jay's political principles for the new nation began with his support of constitutional government. Having labored to put the Constitution in place, Jay believed it—rather than the loudest voices in a mob—should be the guiding principle of American government. Using an extended metaphor, he told his friend William Vaughan:

> I should not think that man wise, who should employ his time in endeavouring to contrive a shoe that would fit every foot; and they do not appear to me much more wise, who expect to devise a government that would suit every nation. I have no objections to men's mending or changing their own shoes, but object to their insisting on mending or changing mine.

In contrast to the utopian schemes of the French Revolution, Jay was quite content with the constitutional "shoe" produced in 1787, believing the political cobblers had done their job well. Foreign interference was unwelcome, especially from those who did not know American circumstances or who offered ideologically "pre-cut" soles. Jay approved of occasional constitutional amendment, but only when it was prudent and well thought out. Reform was best done gradually.

Jay believed democracy was necessary in a constitutional republic, but it should be tempered and bounded. As he told a friend, "Too many . . . love pure democracy dearly. They seem not to consider that pure democracy, like pure rum, easily produces intoxication, and with it a thousand mad pranks and fooleries." He preferred an orderly society with its tone set by "sober and discreet" men. Supporting such an orderly society was morality and religious belief, and Jay came to believe increasingly in the importance of religious faith in the new republic. Finally, Jay hoped that such an orderly society would allow for the cultural and moral improvement of its citizens. If the country followed these guidelines, Jay believed the result would be a successful, flourishing republic.

Jay retired to his country home in Bedford, Westchester County. There he had much time to reflect on the Revolutionary era. His lifelong Protestant Christian beliefs also grew more pronounced in retirement. Faith helped him deal with the loss of both his wife and a daughter. It also impelled Jay to a different type of service: the presidency of the American Bible Society. The American Bible Society was committed to blanketing the nation with the Protestant Scriptures, to be printed "without note or comment," as a means of converting the country. Jay presided over the organization—even though he had little to do with its daily operation—from 1821 to 1825. He died peacefully in 1829, having outlived all the Founders except Charles Carroll.

With such an extended and significant service, Jay's status as a "forgotten" Founder is shocking. As the historian Wilfred McClay observed, "Given the astonishing range of his accomplishment . . . it is amazing that Jay is so little known. He deserves better." Historian R. B. Bernstein suggested that this lack of recognition came about because Jay never signed any of the major Founding documents. Biographer Walter Stahr argued that Jay was more conservative and more religious than many of the other Founders, which explains the lack of attention he has received. I would add that Jay's association with the Federalist Party has hurt him. He was a central figure in a political party that had disappeared by 1820, thus having failed to create a party tradition in which Jay could be remembered. Whatever the case, it is indisputable that without Jay's many services to the new nation, the United States would have lacked a great, effective talent and may have taken a very different course than it did. Jay helped set the nation on a path of stable, constitutional, nonrevolutionary political development.

MAIN CONTRIBUTIONS OF JOHN JAY

Jay forcefully advocated for the ratification of the Constitution. He joined with Alexander Hamilton and James Madison to write the *Federalist Papers*. He also penned the significant "Address to the People of the State of New-York, on the Subject of the Constitution."

Jay served as the first chief justice of the United States. As chief justice, he worked to strengthen the federal government's powers in relation to the states and foreign nations.

Jay acted as President Washington's emissary to Great Britain in 1794–1795. He negotiated the Jay Treaty, which kept the United States out of war with Britain by addressing several areas of tension between the two nations.

From the Pen of John Jay

Nothing is more certain than the indispensable necessity of government, and it is equally undeniable, that whenever and however it is instituted, the people must cede to it some of their natural rights in order to vest it with requisite powers. It is well worthy of consideration therefore, whether it would conduce more to the interest of the people of America that they should, to all general purposes, be one nation, under one federal government, or that they should divide themselves into separate confederacies, and give to the head of each the same kind of powers which they are advised to place in one national government.

It has until lately been a received and uncontradicted opinion that the prosperity of the people of America depended on their continuing firmly united, and the wishes, prayers, and efforts of our best and wisest citizens have been constantly directed to that object. But politicians now appear, who insist that this opinion is erroneous, and that instead of looking for safety and happiness in union, we ought to seek it in a division of the States into distinct confederacies or sovereignties. However extraordinary this new doctrine may appear, it nevertheless has its advocates; and certain characters who were much opposed to it formerly, are at present of the number. Whatever may be the arguments or inducements which have wrought this change in the sentiments and declarations of these gentlemen, it certainly would not be wise in the people at large to adopt these new political tenets without being fully convinced that they are founded in truth and sound policy.

It has often given me pleasure to observe that independent America was not composed of detached and distant territories, but that one connected, fertile, widespreading country was the portion of our western sons of liberty. Providence has in a particular manner blessed it with a variety of soils and productions, and watered it with innumerable streams, for the delight and accommodation of its inhabitants. A succession of navigable waters forms a kind of chain round its borders, as if to bind it together; while the most noble rivers in the world, running at convenient distances, present them with highways for the easy communication of friendly aids, and the mutual transportation and exchange of their various commodities.

With equal pleasure I have as often taken notice that Providence has been pleased to give this one connected country to one united people—a people descended from the same ancestors, speaking the same language, professing the same religion, attached to the same principles of government, very similar in their manners and customs, and who, by their joint counsels, arms, and efforts, fighting side by side throughout a long and bloody war, have nobly established general liberty and independence.

This country and this people seem to have been made for each other, and it appears as if it was the design of Providence, that an inheritance so proper and convenient for a band of brethren, united to each other by the strongest ties, should never be split into a number of unsocial, jealous, and alien sovereignties.

Similar sentiments have hitherto prevailed among all orders and denominations of men among us. To all general purposes we have uniformly been one people each individual citizen everywhere enjoying the same national rights, privileges, and protection. As a nation we have made peace and war; as a nation we have vanquished our common enemies; as a nation we have formed alliances, and made treaties, and entered into various compacts and conventions with foreign states.

A strong sense of the value and blessings of union induced the people, at a very early period, to institute a federal government to preserve and perpetuate it. . . .

This [Constitutional] convention, composed of men who possessed the confidence of the people, and many of whom had become highly distinguished by their patriotism, virtue and wisdom, in times which tried the minds and hearts of men, undertook the arduous task. In the mild season of peace, with minds unoccupied by other subjects, they passed many months in cool, uninterrupted, and daily consultation; and finally, without having been awed by power, or influenced by any passions except love for their country, they presented and recommended to the people the plan produced by their joint and very unanimous councils. . . .

It is worthy of remark that not only the first, but every succeeding Congress, as well as the late convention, have invariably joined with the people in thinking that the prosperity of America depended on its Union. To preserve and perpetuate it was the great object of the people in forming that convention, and it is also the great object of the plan which the convention has advised them to adopt. With what propriety, therefore, or for what good purposes, are attempts at this particular period made by some men to depreciate the importance of the Union? Or why is it suggested that three or four confederacies would be better than one? I am persuaded in my own mind that the people have always thought right on this subject, and that their universal and uniform attachment to the cause of the Union rests on great and weighty reasons, which I shall endeavor to develop and explain in some ensuing papers. They who promote the idea of substituting a number of distinct confederacies in the room of the plan of the convention, seem clearly to foresee that the rejection of it would put the continuance of the Union in the utmost jeopardy. That certainly would be the case, and I sincerely wish that it may be as clearly foreseen by every good citizen, that whenever the dissolution of the Union arrives, America will have reason to exclaim, in the words of the poet: "FAREWELL! A LONG FAREWELL TO ALL MY GREATNESS."

—John Jay, *Federalist Papers*, Number 2 (1787)

Recommended Reading

Walter Stahr, *John Jay: Founding Father* (New York: Hambledon and London, 2005).

Richard B. Morris, *Witnesses at the Creation: Hamilton, Madison, Jay, and the Constitution* (New York: Holt, Rinehart, and Winston, 1985).

Todd Estes, *The Jay Treaty Debate, Public Opinion, and the Evolution of Early American Political Culture* (Amherst: University of Massachusetts Press, 2006).

The John Jay Papers Project. http://www.columbia.edu/cu/lweb/digital/jay.

"Philosophy may mislead you. Ask experience."

    —*Roger Sherman,* Countryman V, *December 20, 1787*

"Minorities talk; majorities vote."

    —*Roger Sherman*

ROGER SHERMAN
(1721–1793)

MARK DAVID HALL

Roger Sherman was the only Founder to help draft and sign the Declaration and Resolves (1774), the Articles of Association (1774), the Declaration of Independence (1776), the Articles of Confederation (1777, 1778), and the U.S. Constitution (1787). He served more days in the Continental Congress than all but four men, and he was on the five-man committee that wrote the Declaration of Independence. At the Constitutional Convention of 1787, he spoke more than all but three delegates and was the driving force behind the Connecticut Compromise. As a representative and senator in the national legislature under the U.S. Constitution, he played critical roles in debates over the Bill of Rights, the assumption of state debts, and the establishment of a national bank. Even as he was helping to create and run a new nation, he served simultaneously in a variety of state offices.

ROGER SHERMAN WAS BORN IN STOUGHTON, MASSACHUSETTS, IN 1721. Shortly after the death of his father in 1741, he moved to

"Sherman is the only person to have signed all the essential documents of the American Founding. That includes the Declaration of Independence, the Articles of Confederation, the Constitution, and the Bill of Rights. He was instrumental in both moderating Madison's nationalism at the Constitutional Convention and securing ratification of the Constitution and the Bill of Rights."

—Gordon Lloyd

New Milford, Connecticut, where he worked as a cobbler, surveyor, and store owner. Sherman never went to college, but he was a voracious reader. He taught himself advanced mathematics, and in 1750 he began publishing a popular almanac that was issued annually or biannually until 1761. Sherman later studied law and was admitted to the Litchfield bar in 1754. As he prospered professionally, he was selected for a variety of local offices and was elected to several six-month terms in the lower house of Connecticut's General Assembly.

In 1760, after the death of his first wife (with whom he had seven children), Sherman moved to New Haven. He opened a store next to Yale College and sold general merchandise, provisions, and books. Sherman married Rebecca Prescott three years later, and they had eight children. He was again elected to the lower house of the General Assembly, and in 1766 Connecticut voters chose him to be one of the twelve members of the upper house, or Council of Assistants. Traditionally, four assistants were selected by the General Assembly to serve with the deputy governor as the judges on Connecticut's Superior Court. Sherman was appointed to this court in 1766, and he held both offices until he resigned from the legislature in 1785. He remained a superior court judge until he became a member of the United States House of Representatives in 1789.

Beginning with the Stamp Act crisis of 1765, Sherman was a consistent opponent of what he considered to be British abuses of power. As a member of the First Continental Congress in 1774, he helped draft and signed the Declaration and Resolves, which among other things declared:

> That the inhabitants of the English Colonies in North America, by the immutable laws of nature, the principles of the English constitution, and the several charters or compacts, have the following Rights:
> *Resolved:* 1. That they are entitled to life, liberty, and property, and they have never ceded to any sovereign power whatever, a right to dispose of either without their consent. . . .

The Congress went on to assert that Parliament had no authority to tax the colonies, although to Sherman's chagrin it conceded that it could regulate colonial trade.

In addition to declaring their rights and petitioning the king, the First Continental Congress passed the Articles of Association, whereby delegates agreed on behalf of their colonies not to import and consume goods from Great Britain or Ireland. The articles provided for the creation of committees in each county, city, and town to enforce the terms of the association. Sherman signed this agreement, and he later was moderator at the New Haven town meeting that formed the committee to implement the articles in that city. He occasionally chaired this body, but pressing responsibilities in Congress necessitated frequent absences from New Haven.

In 1776, Sherman was the only delegate to serve on all three of the most important congressional committees: the Board of War, the committee to draft the Declaration of Independence (fellow members included Thomas Jefferson, John Adams, Benjamin Franklin, and Robert Livingston), and the thirteen-member committee to draft what became the Articles of Confederation. He was intimately involved with the war effort and in writing the Articles, but unfortunately for his future fame, he was content for Jefferson to do most of the work on the Declaration. He was repeatedly selected to represent his state in the Continental and Confederation congresses, eventually serving a total of 1,543 days.

Back in Connecticut, Sherman and the aptly named Richard Law accepted the task of revising *all* of Connecticut's statutes. To divide this huge endeavor, Sherman took statutes beginning with the letters *A* through *L*, and Law took the rest. The two worked on the project throughout the summer and fall of 1783. The General Assembly reviewed their work and approved it with a few changes in January 1784. Among Sherman's contributions was a religious- liberty statute entitled "An Act for securing the Rights of Conscience in Matters of Religion, to Christians of every Denomination in this State." The revisions also included a law providing for the gradual emancipation of children born to slaves in Connecticut after March 1, 1784.

In 1787 the General Assembly appointed Sherman, Oliver Ellsworth, and William Samuel Johnson to represent Connecticut in the Constitutional Convention. No delegate had more experience in national government and only one member—Benjamin Franklin—had more experience in politics than Sherman. In spite of his age, he spoke more than all but three delegates.

Sherman arrived in Philadelphia convinced that the national government's powers needed to be strengthened, but he was also a firm supporter of both local and limited government. As such, he was shocked by Madison's proposals for a national legislature based upon proportional representation and possessing a general grant of power and the ability to veto state laws. Sherman tenaciously fought each of these ideas, eventually winning equal representation for states in the Senate, an enumeration of Congress's powers, and the elimination of the national government's ability to veto state laws. He was less successful in his opposition to a single, powerful executive who would be independent of the legislature.

Sherman's most significant contribution in Philadelphia was the "Great," or "Connecticut," Compromise. When it became apparent that the large states would not accept retaining the Articles' provision of one state, one vote, and the small states would not agree to proportional representation alone, Sherman helped craft the compromise whereby membership in the House of Representatives would be proportionally allocated based on state population, while states would be represented equally in the Senate—initially with the senators to be chosen by the state legislatures. Without this compromise, it is unlikely the Constitution would have been ratified.

Sherman's contributions in the Constitutional Convention were neglected for many years, but scholars have recently gained a better appreciation for them. For instance, David Brian Robertson concludes in a 2005 article published in *American Political Science Review* (the discipline's top journal) that Sherman often outmaneuvered Madison at the Constitutional Convention, and he suggests that the "political synergy between Madison and Sherman . . . very well may have been necessary for the Constitution's adoption."

After the Convention, Sherman returned to Connecticut, where he wrote seven newspaper essays under the pseudonyms of "Countryman" and "A Citizen of New Haven" defending the Constitution. He was elected to represent New Haven at the state ratification convention where, according to one account, "all the objections to the Constitution vanished before the learning and eloquence of a Johnson, the genuine good sense and discernment of a Sherman, and the Demosthenian energy of an Ellsworth." The reporter may have been biased, but the sense of Federalist domination was accurate as indicated by the January 9, 1788, vote of 128–40 in favor of the Constitution. Connecticut thus became the fifth state to ratify the document.

In December of 1788, Sherman was elected to the House of Representatives, and in 1791 he was appointed to the U.S. Senate to fill the unexpired term of William Samuel Johnson. In Congress he engaged in debates over tariffs, the assumption of state debts, and the creation of a national bank. Although initially opposed to adding a bill of rights to the Constitution, Sherman served on the eleven-member House committee that drafted the amendments, was an active participant in debates over the specific provisions, and was a member of the six-person conference committee that put the amendments into their final form. Sherman also argued for placing the amendments after the original Constitution rather than interspersing them within the text, as originally proposed by Madison. Sherman remained active in politics until his death on July 23, 1793.

> "No individual was more directly and intimately involved in the major actions of the American Founding than Roger Sherman."
>
> —Daniel L. Dreisbach

Sherman was held in high esteem by his contemporaries. In 1777, John Adams described him as "that old puritan, as honest as an angel, and as firm in the cause of American Independence as Mt. Atlas." Late in life, Patrick Henry remarked that Sherman and George Mason were "the greatest statesmen he ever knew."

Thomas Jefferson, who was often at odds with both Adams and Henry, shared their admiration for Sherman. He once pointed Sherman out to a visitor and noted, "That is Mr. Sherman of Connecticut, a man who never said a foolish thing in his life."

Jefferson's comment highlights Sherman's proclivity to bring a healthy dose of common sense to political deliberations. In the Constitutional Convention, Robert Yates recorded him as commenting: "I am not fond of speculation. I would rather proceed on experimental ground [i.e., on the ground of experience]." Similarly, in an essay defending the proposed Constitution, Sherman wrote, "Philosophy may mislead you. Ask experience." His contributions to crafting the Declaration and Resolves (1774), the Articles of Association (1774), the Declaration of Independence (1776), the Articles of Confederation (1777, 1778), the U.S. Constitution (1787), and the Bill of Rights (1789) all reflect his prudential approach to politics.

Sherman was not a radical thinker, a great author, or a stirring orator—realities that diminished his contemporary and future fame. Nevertheless, as historian Jack N. Rakove comments in his Pulitzer Prize–winning book *Original Meanings*, "America has had more Shermans in its politics than Madisons, and arguably too few of either, but it was the rivalry between their competing goals and political styles that jointly gave the Great Convention much of its drama and fascination—and also permitted its achievement." Scholars, teachers, and students who wish to understand America's Founding cannot afford to ignore the contributions of that old Connecticut Puritan, Roger Sherman.

Main Contributions of Roger Sherman

Sherman was the only person to sign the Declaration and Resolves (1774), the Articles of Association (1774), the Declaration of Independence (1776), the Articles of Confederation (1777, 1778), and the U.S. Constitution (1787).

Sherman played critical roles in drafting the Constitution and the Bill of Rights.

Sherman was actively involved in Connecticut state government, serving in the upper house of the General Assembly from 1766 to 1785 and on the superior court from 1766 to 1789. In 1783 he and Richard Law revised all of Connecticut's laws.

From the Pen of Roger Sherman

As the happiness of a People, and the good Order of Civil Society, essentially depend upon Piety, Religion and Morality, it is the Duty of the Civil Authority to provide for the Support and Encouragement thereof; so as that Christians of every Denomination, demeaning themselves peaceably, and as good Subjects of the State, may be equally under the Protection of the Laws: And as the People of this State have in general, been of one Profession in Matters of Faith, religious Worship, and the mode of settling and supporting the Ministers of the Gospel, they have by Law been formed into Ecclesiastical Societies, for the more convenient Support of their Worship and Ministry: And to the End that other Denominations of Christians who dissent from the Worship and Ministry so established and supported, may enjoy free Liberty of Conscience in the Matters aforesaid:

Be it enacted by the Governor, Council and Representatives, in General Court assembled, and by the Authority of the same, That no Persons in this State, professing the Christian Religion, who soberly and conscientiously dissent from the Worship and Ministry by Law established in the Society wherein they dwell, and attend public Worship by themselves, shall incur any Penalty for not attending the Worship and Ministry so established, on the Lord's-Day, or on account of their meeting together by themselves on said Day, for public Worship in a Way agreeable to their Consciences.

And be it further enacted by the Authority aforesaid, That all denominations of Christians differing in their religious Sentiments from the People of the established Societies in this State, whether of the Episcopal Church, or those Congregationalists called Separates, or of the People called Baptists, or Quakers, or any other Denomination who shall have formed themselves into distinct Churches or Congregations, and attend public Worship, and support the gospel Ministry in a Way agreeable to their Consciences and respective Professions; and all Persons who adhere to any of them, and dwell so near to any Place of their Worship that they can do ordinarily attend the same on the Sabbath, and contribute their due Proportion to the support of the Worship and Ministry where they so attend, whether such Place of Worship be within this, or any adjoining State, and produce a Certificate thereof from such Church or Congregation, signed by their Order, by the Minister or other Officer thereof, and lodge the same with the Clerk of the Society wherein such Person or Persons dwell, every such Person shall be exempted from being taxed for the support of the Worship and Ministry of said Society, so long as he or they shall continue so to attend and support public Worship with a different Church or Congregation as aforesaid.

And be it further enacted by the Authority aforesaid, That all such Protestant Churches and Congregations as different from the Worship and Ministry established as aforesaid, and who maintain and attend public Worship by themselves, shall have Liberty and Authority to use and exercise the same Powers and Privileges for maintaining and supporting their respective Ministers, and building and repairing their Meeting-Houses for the public Worship of God, as the Ecclesiastical Societies, constituted by Act of the

General Assembly of this State by Law have and do exercise and enjoy; and in the same Manner may commence and hold their Meetings, and transact their Affairs, as Occasion may require for the Purpose aforesaid.

And all Persons shall be taxed for the support of the Ministry and other Charges of the Society wherein they dwell, who do not attend and help Support, any other public Worship; any thing in this Act notwithstanding.

And every Person claiming the benefit of this Act, shall be disqualified to vote in any Society Meeting, save only for granting Taxes for the support of Schools, and for the Establishment of Rules and Regulations for Schools, and the Education of Children in them.

—Roger Sherman, from "An Act for securing the Rights of Conscience in Matters of Religion, to Christians of every Denomination in this State" (1784)

Recommended Reading

Christopher Collier, *Roger Sherman's Connecticut: Yankee Politics and the American Revolution* (Middletown, CT: Wesleyan University Press, 1971).

Mark David Hall, "Roger Sherman: An Old Puritan in a New Nation," in *The Forgotten Founders on Religion and Public Life*, ed. Daniel L. Dreisbach, Mark David Hall, and Jeffry H. Morrison (Notre Dame: University of Notre Dame Press, 2009), 248–77.

Scott Gerber, "Roger Sherman and the Bill of Rights," *Polity* 28 (Summer 1996): 521–40.

"It is a proposition too plain to be contested, that the constitution controls any legislative act repugnant to it. . . . [A]n act of the legislature repugnant to the constitution is void. . . . It is emphatically the province and duty of the judicial department to say what the law is."

—*John Marshall,* Marbury v. Madison *(1803)*

"The government of the United States, then, though limited in its powers, is supreme; and its laws, when made in pursuance of the constitution, form the supreme law of the land, 'any thing in the constitution or laws of any State to the contrary notwithstanding.'"

—*John Marshall,* McCulloch v. Maryland *(1819)*

"This power [over commerce], like all others vested in congress, is complete in itself, may be exercised to its utmost extent, and acknowledges no limitations, other than are prescribed in the constitution. . . . If, as has always been understood, the sovereignty of congress, though limited to specified objects, is plenary as to those objects, the power over commerce with foreign nations, and among the several states, is vested in congress as absolutely as it would be in a single government."

—*John Marshall,* Gibbons v. Ogden *(1824)*

JOHN MARSHALL
(1755–1835)

HENRY J. ABRAHAM and BARBARA A. PERRY

Matthew J. Franck has summarized John Marshall brilliantly: "A brave soldier in the Revolution, a brilliant lawyer, a leader in Virginia's ratification of the Constitution, an accomplished diplomat, congressman, and secretary of state, John Marshall could have retired from public life in 1801 with a secure though minor place in the tale of the early Republic. But for the next three and a half decades, as chief justice of the United States, he had a more profound impact on American life than any other judge in our history. He established the Supreme Court's independence as a coequal branch of government, enunciated and defended the essential principles of the American Union, and taught his contemporaries and posterity alike how to read and understand the United States Constitution—a task that amounted to the completion of the Founding."

ONE OF THE FIRST ACTIONS JOHN G. ROBERTS JR. TOOK AFTER BEING sworn in as chief justice in 2005 was to send an emissary to Richmond, Virginia, on a mission to procure John Marshall's judicial robe, displayed at his historic home. Roberts wanted to replicate the garment worn by his hero, known as the Great Chief Justice. The Supreme Court's new leader could not have chosen a better role model on whom to pattern his attire or tenure.

Born near Germantown in 1755, on the frontier of colonial Virginia, John Marshall was the eldest of fifteen children. His parents and tutors provided most of young John's early education, but his schooling in human nature as the oldest sibling of such a large brood taught him leadership skills that would last a lifetime. Following the "shot heard round the world," at Lexington and Concord, which launched the American Revolution in 1775, Marshall and his father enlisted with the Culpeper Minute Men. John later served with a Virginia Continental Regiment, rising to the rank of captain. He led his men in the battles of Great Bridge, Brandywine, Germantown, and Monmouth Courthouse. He also suffered through the winter encampment at Valley Forge, emerging with a life-long admiration for George Washington, about whom he wrote a five-volume biography entitled *Life of George Washington*.

After the War for Independence, Marshall studied with the renowned legal scholar George Wythe at the College of William and Mary. After acceptance to the bar, Marshall moved to Virginia's capital, Richmond, settling there with his wife, Polly. They had ten children, six of whom survived to adulthood. Blessed with abundant intellectual skills, verbal talents, and charm, Marshall achieved success as an appellate lawyer in state and federal courts. His public service in Virginia's Council of State (1782–1784) and its House of Delegates (1782, 1784–1785, 1787–1788, 1795) con-

"John Marshall played a crucial role at key stages of the Founding."

—Ryan J. Barilleaux

firmed his doubts about the competency of state government. Marshall became a staunch nationalist and member of the Federalist Party, whose views he represented as an elected delegate to the Virginia convention that ratified the new federal Constitution in 1787. His lucid defense of the proposed federal judiciary contributed to the convention's adoption of the national system that governs the United States to this day.

An effective spokesman for President Washington's policies, Marshall received offers to appointive offices, but he rejected them to continue his lucrative law practice. When President John Adams asked him to serve on a diplomatic mission to revolutionary France, however, he accepted. As the United States attempted to maneuver between French and British hostilities, the assignment was particularly delicate. Marshall and his two colleagues, Charles Cotesworth Pinckney and Elbridge Gerry, returned from France as heroes for refusing to pay a bribe to representatives of the French government. As a result, President Washington, now in retirement, prevailed upon Marshall to run for a seat in the U.S. House of Representatives from a Richmond district. He served there for less than a year (1799–1800), presenting moderate Federalist views in House debates.

In 1800, President Adams appointed Marshall secretary of state. During his nine months in the cabinet, his duties included conducting American foreign policy, facilitating appointments to federal offices, and assisting the president in government administration while he was away from the nation's capital.

On January 20, 1801, John Adams, a lame-duck president since his defeat by Thomas Jefferson in 1800, nominated Marshall to serve as chief justice of the United States. One week later, the Senate approved the appointment unanimously, setting the stage for his nearly thirty-five-year tenure on the highest court in the land.

From 1801 to 1835, he wrote 519 out of the 1,215 opinions issued by the Court, including more than half of the sixty-two decisions the justices handed down on constitutional questions. It is simply beyond dispute that Chief Justice Marshall, more than any other individual in the history of the Court, determined the developing character of America's federal constitutional system. He raised the Court from its lowly, if not discredited, position to a level of equality with the executive and the legislative branches, perhaps even to one of dominance during the heyday of his chief justiceship. Long after the Federalist Party had faded from the political scene (John Adams was its last president), Marshall continued to write the party's nationalist philosophy into constitutional law. Adams could proudly and justly say, "My gift of John Marshall to the people of the United States was the proudest act of my life. There is no act of my life on which I reflect with more pleasure. I have given to my country a judge equal to a Hale, a Holt, or a Mansfield."

Marshall handed down four of the most momentous decisions in the nation's history. *Marbury v. Madison* (1803) established the Supreme Court's power of judicial review over congressional acts and solidified the U.S. Constitution's supremacy. Events giving rise to this case began after Thomas Jefferson, a Republican, defeated President Adams's bid for reelection in 1800. Just prior to leaving office, Adams, a staunch Federalist, appointed a number of his party's loyalists to the federal bench. In response, the Jeffersonian Republicans in Congress repealed the Judiciary Act of 1800, which had created new circuit courts and judgeships. By the time Jefferson assumed the presidency, a number of Adams's commissions had been signed but not delivered. President Jefferson ordered his new secretary of state, James Madison, not to deliver them. As a result, William Marbury, one of Adams's nominees who had not received his commission, sued Madison and requested that the

Supreme Court order him to deliver the commission. The Judiciary Act of 1789 provided the Court with authority to deliver this order (called a writ of mandamus). Marshall immediately recognized that the Jefferson administration would ignore the Court's order. On the other hand, failure to grant the writ could be interpreted as a sign of weakness. Ingeniously, Marshall crafted a third way. The Court held that Adams's appointment of Marbury was valid, that Madison should have delivered Marbury's commission, but that Marbury had no legal remedy because the Court's authority to issue writs of mandamus was unconstitutional because this power was outside the authority granted to it by the Constitution. Marshall turned a no-win situation into one of the most masterful judicial power plays of all time. By proclaiming that "[it] is emphatically the province and duty of the judicial department to say what the law is," Marshall's opinion in *Marbury* ensured the Supreme Court's coequal status in relation to the Congress and the president. In addition, the landmark decision confirmed the U.S. Constitution as the supreme law of the land.

McCulloch v. Maryland (1819) arose from the state of Maryland's attempts to impede the business of the Second Bank of the United States by placing a tax on every note it issued. McCulloch, a Second Bank cashier, refused to pay the tax. Two significant constitutional questions resulted from the impasse. First, did Congress have the authority to establish/reestablish the bank? Second, if Congress did possess this power, did the Maryland law unconstitutionally interfere with that power? Marshall concluded that although Congress did not have the enumerated power to create a national bank, it, likewise, was not explicitly prohibited from such action. Further, he determined that because Congress did have certain enumerated powers, such as to lay and collect taxes and raise armies, it would also need the means to complete these tasks. The

> *"He had a more profound impact on American life than any other judge in our history. He established the Supreme Court's independence as a coequal branch of government, enunciated and defended the essential principles of the American Union, and taught his contemporaries and posterity alike how to read and understand the United States Constitution—a task that amounted to the completion of the Founding."*
>
> —Matthew J. Franck

law chartering the Second Bank was a "necessary and proper" one (granted in Article I, Section 19 of the Constitution), which would allow Congress to act on its enumerated powers. Thus, Marshall's opinion in *McCulloch* reaffirmed the Constitution as the supreme law of the land, thereby making state law subordinate. As such, the Second Bank was a legitimate federal institution immune from the state's sovereign powers (including taxation). In expanding Congress's implied power, Marshall also strengthened the authority of the national government.

In another of Marshall's most momentous decisions, *Dartmouth College v. Woodward* (1819), the Supreme Court afforded private parties protection from state and legislative interference. This case arose, much like *Marbury v. Madison*, as a result of the political differences between the Federalists and the Jeffersonian Republicans. In 1818, Jefferson's party governed New Hampshire. The newly elected governor and legislature, unhappy with the Federalist trustees at Dartmouth College, attempted to oust them and remake the college into a university under state control. Marshall concluded that the college was a private institution. As such, he viewed the charter of Dartmouth College as a contract between a private entity and the state. The Constitution's Contract Clause, therefore, protected this private entity from state interference.

Marshall's ruling placed a significant limitation on states' authority to regulate and interfere with private corporations.

Gibbons v. Ogden (1824) completes the historic quartet of decisions penned by Marshall. The case arose as a result of New York's attempts to regulate steamboat travel on its waterways. Thomas Gibbons held a federal coasting license that allowed him to travel between New Jersey and New York. Aaron Ogden held the state-required license. Gibbons contended that he was not required to pay any fees to New York because the federal license trumped any state license. Marshall implemented the Constitution's Supremacy Clause and concluded that Congress had the exclusive right to control interstate and foreign commerce. Once again, Marshall's jurisprudence served to strengthen the federal government's power.

Justice Benjamin Cardozo, who served briefly but brilliantly on the Supreme Court in the 1930s, wrote, "Marshall gave to the Constitution of the United States the impress of his own mind; and the form of our constitutional law is what it is, because he molded it while it was still plastic and malleable in the fire of his own intense convictions." "Those organ tones of his," he wrote elsewhere, "were meant to fill cathedrals." The Marshall Court led the federal government and gave it the means to develop and work. Lord Bryce, close student of American democracy and Britain's ambassador to the United States from 1907 to 1913, spoke of Marshall's decisions as "never having been surpassed and rarely equaled by the most famous jurists of modern Europe or of ancient Rome." When the Great Chief Justice died in 1835, his death hastened by a stagecoach accident he suffered while riding judicial circuit, one newspaper eulogized, "Next to [George] Washington, only, did he possess the reverence and the homage of the heart of the American people."

Main Contributions of John Marshall

Marshall bolstered the power of the U.S. Supreme Court, particularly by establishing the power of judicial review, and made it a coequal branch of the federal government.

Marshall broadly interpreted Congress's implied power and declared it supreme over state authority. His interpretation that Congress's interstate commerce power is plenary set the stage for the national government's economic hegemony.

As the fourth chief justice of the United States, from 1801 to 1835, Marshall established the model of leadership for his successors on the nation's highest tribunal.

From the Pen of
John Marshall

That the people have an original right to establish, for their future government, such principles as, in their opinion, shall most conduce to their own happiness, is the basis on which the whole American fabric has been erected. The exercise of this original right is a very great exertion; nor can it, nor ought it, to be frequently repeated. The principles, therefore, so established, are deemed fundamental. And as the authority from which they proceed, is supreme, and can seldom act, they are designed to be permanent.

This original and supreme will organizes the government, and assigns, to different departments, their respective powers. It may either stop here; or establish certain limits not to be transcended by those departments.

The government of the United States is of the latter description. The powers of the legislature are defined, and limited; and that those limits may not be mistaken, or forgotten, the constitution is written. To what purpose are powers limited, and to what purpose is the limitation committed to writing, if these limits may, at any time, be passed by those intended to be restrained? The distinction, between a government with limited and unlimited powers, is abolished, if those limits do not confine the persons on whom they are imposed, and if acts prohibited and acts allowed, are of equal obligation. It is a proposition too plain to be contested, that the constitution controls any legislative act repugnant to it; or, that the legislature may alter the constitution by an ordinary act.

Between these alternatives there is no middle ground. The constitution is either superior, paramount law, unchangeable by ordinary means, or it is on a level with ordinary legislative acts, and, like other acts, is alterable when the legislature shall please to alter it.

If the former part of the alternative be true, then a legislative act contrary to the constitution is not law: if the latter part be true, then written constitutions are absurd attempts, on the part of the people, to limit a power, in its own nature illimitable.

Certainly all those who have framed written constitutions contemplate them as forming the fundamental and paramount law of the nation, and consequently the theory of every such government must be, that an act of the legislature, repugnant to the constitution, is void.

This theory is essentially attached to a written constitution, and is, consequently to be considered by this court, as one of the fundamental principles of our society. It is not therefore to be lost sight of in the future consideration of this subject. . . .

It is emphatically the province and duty of the judicial department to say what the law is. Those who apply the rule to particular cases, must of necessity expound and interpret that rule. If two laws conflict with each other, the courts must decide on the operation of each.

—John Marshall, *Marbury v. Madison* (1803)

Recommended Reading

Herbert A. Johnson, "John Marshall, 1801–1835," in Clare Cushman, ed., *The Supreme Court Justices: Illustrated Biographies, 1789–1995* (Washington, DC: Congressional Quarterly, 1995).

R. Kent Newmyer, *John Marshall and the Heroic Age of the Supreme Court* (Baton Rouge: Louisiana State University, 2001).

James F. Simon, *What Kind of Nation: Thomas Jefferson, John Marshall, and the Epic Struggle to Create a United States* (New York: Simon & Schuster, 2002).

Jean Edward Smith, *John Marshall: Definer of a Nation* (New York: Henry Holt, 1996).

"For WHO ARE A FREE PEOPLE? Not *those*, over whom government is reasonable and equitably exercised, but *those*, who live under a government so *constitutionally checked and controlled*, that proper provision is made against its being otherwise exercised."

—*John Dickinson, Letter VII,* Letters from a Farmer in Pennsylvania

"Let these *truths* be indelibly impressed on our minds—*that* we *cannot be* HAPPY, *without being* FREE—that we cannot be free, *without being secure in our property*—that *we* cannot be secure in our property, *if, without our consent, others may, as by right, take it away. . . .*"

—*John Dickinson, Letter XII,* Letters from a Farmer in Pennsylvania

"Experience must be our only guide. Reason may mislead us."

—*John Dickinson, Speech at the Constitutional Convention, August 13, 1787*

JOHN DICKINSON
(1732–1808)

HOWARD L. LUBERT

When, on July 2, 1776, John Dickinson abstained from the congressional vote on independence from Great Britain, he was not unaware of the effect his decision would have on his reputation. "My conduct this day I expect will give the finishing blow to my once too great, and, my integrity considered, now too diminished popularity." Yet Dickinson's diminished fame does not accurately reflect the important role he played in America's Founding. Rightly dubbed the "penman of the Revolution," he played as significant a political role during the imperial crisis with Great Britain (1764–1776) as anyone. More, he remained politically relevant after independence, helping to frame the Articles of Confederation, playing a notable role at the 1787 Constitutional Convention, and writing well-received essays in favor of the Constitution drafted by that Convention.

JOHN DICKINSON WAS BORN IN TALBOT COUNTY, MARYLAND, IN November 1732. When he was eight years old, his family moved, settling near Dover, Delaware. After being privately tutored, in 1750 Dickinson began to study law under John Moland in Philadelphia. He completed his legal studies in London at Middle Temple, one of England's four great Inns of Court. He returned to Philadelphia in 1757, where he began a successful law practice. He soon entered politics, serving in the Delaware and Pennsylvania assemblies (1760–1765), where, according to a fellow assemblyman, Dickinson "greatly distinguished himself . . . as an orator."

Dickinson's first significant public act was to argue in May of 1764 against a proposal to ask King George III to replace Pennsylvania's proprietary government with a royal government. The plan, sponsored in part by Benjamin Franklin, a leader of the Popular, or Quaker, Party, sought to limit the broad political power of the colony's proprietors (the Penn family) and to subject their lands to the same taxes paid by the rest of the colony's residents. Dickinson found the Penn family's claim of exemption from taxes "fundamentally unjust" and "contradictory to the maxims of equity; and the spirit of liberty." But when Franklin, who had long desired to see the proprietary government replaced, urged the assembly to ask for a revocation of the colony's charter, Dickinson broke with him. While Dickinson was not an advocate of the proprietary government, he questioned the "fatal speed" with which the assembly was moving. Further, he challenged the assumption that replacing the current government with a royal one could be accomplished without threatening crucial privileges—including religious liberty, the "best and greatest of all rights"—which the colony enjoyed under its 1701 Charter of Privileges. The summer and fall of 1764 were marked by a bitter newspaper war between Dickinson, on the one hand, and leaders of the Popular Party, principally Joseph Galloway, on the other. When elections were held on October 1, Dickinson was reelected, and Franklin and Galloway were defeated.

However, the Popular Party still controlled the assembly, and as that body moved forward with its plan to ask the king for a change of government, Dickinson decided that he would not seek reelection in October 1765.

Dickinson remained active in politics, taking the lead in formulating the colonial response to Parliament's passage of the Stamp Act (1765). In the process, he earned a reputation throughout the colonies as a Patriot as well as a thoughtful and articulate spokesman for the colonists' cause. The Pennsylvania assembly selected Dickinson as a delegate to the Stamp Act Congress in New York (October 1765), where he was the main author of the Congress's resolutions against the act. In November he published *The Late Regulations Respecting the British Colonies on the Continent of America Considered*, which was printed in London the following year. *The Late Regulations* contended that the Stamp Act would hurt the

> "Dickinson was one of the most admired and respected statesman and writers of his time in the colonies and early American Republic. . . . His influence and eloquence are the best arguments against the rationalist Enlightenment view of the American Founding."
>
> —E. Christian Kopff

prosperity of Great Britain and her colonies and, according to one London critic, was "highly esteemed" by the British public and "gained for the author much reputation." In other essays he wrote at the time, including *Friends and Countrymen* (1765) and *An Address to the Committee of Correspondence in Barbados* (1766), Dickinson defended the rights of the colonists and sketched out a constitutional argument about the nature of the empire and the corresponding limits to Parliament's authority.

Parliament's repeal of the Stamp Act in 1766 momentarily returned the colonies to a state of normalcy, but its passage of the Townshend Acts in June 1767, along with the Restraining Act suspending the New York legislature, rekindled Dickinson's fear that colonial liberties were increasingly in danger. Determined to sound the alarm, he adopted the persona of a common Pennsylvania farmer and began to write *Letters from a Farmer in Pennsylvania: To the Inhabitants of the British Colonies*. The first of these essays was published on December 2, 1767, and he continued to write one "letter" a week for twelve weeks. Although they were published under a pseudonym, Dickinson's authorship became public knowledge in May 1768. The letters' importance was recognized immediately. Two days after publication of the first essay in the *Pennsylvania Chronicle and Universal Advisor*, it was reprinted in two other state newspapers. Ultimately, nineteen of the colonies' twenty-three newspapers printed all twelve of the *Farmer's Letters*. In March 1768, the first pamphlet version of the *Letters* was published, constituting one of seven separate editions that would be printed in the colonies in 1768 and 1769. Those years also saw publication of editions in London and Dublin and a French translation in Paris. In addition to his essays, Dickinson wrote a popular Patriotic anthem, "The Liberty Song," which was published in the *Boston Gazette* in July 1768 and later that year appeared in the *Boston Chronicle*. It was in this song that Dickinson coined the phrase "By uniting we stand, by dividing we fall," a rallying cry that was used after the attacks of September 11, 2001.

It is difficult to overstate the influence of Dickinson's *Farmer's Letters*. Until Thomas Paine published *Common Sense* in early 1776, no colonial publication received more praise or was more widely read than these essays. As Milton Flower noted in his biography of Dickinson, "Until the year of Independence, John Dickinson, apart from Benjamin Franklin, was probably the American known to more colonists than any other. Indeed, between the years of the Stamp Act crisis and the convening of the Second Continental Congress (1765–1775), Dickinson was widely recognized as the chief spokesman for American rights and liberty." Public praise flowed in all forms. The College of New Jersey (Princeton) gave him an honorary degree in 1769. Paul Revere engraved a portrait plate of Dickinson for a 1772 almanac. Patience Wright, the wax sculptor, added Dickinson's likeness to her collection. And in 1783, Dickinson College in Pennsylvania was chartered in his honor.

In response to Parliament's Tea Act of 1773, Dickinson again took up the pen to urge Americans to resist an unjust law. In July 1774, after the Boston Tea Party the previous December and the subsequent passage by Parliament of the harsh Boston Port Act, Dickinson drafted for the Provincial Convention of Pennsylvania a set of resolutions against the act, along with a long statement explaining why Parliament's actions were unconstitutional. That long statement was published separately as *An Essay on the Constitutional Power of Great-Britain over the Colonies in America* (1774). Then, as a delegate to the first Continental Congress, Dickinson drafted Congress's *Address to the Inhabitants of Quebec* and the *Petition to the King.*

When the Second Continental Congress convened in May 1775, Dickinson was again among the delegates. He penned drafts of Congress's "Olive Branch" petition and the Declaration of the Causes and Necessity of Taking Up Arms. He also chaired the committee charged with drafting articles of union and produced the first working draft of those articles. But after the battles of Lexington and Concord in April 1775, Dickinson's desire for reconciliation with Great Britain was less and less politically tenable. In Congress, the forces promoting independence grew dominant, particularly after Thomas Paine published *Common Sense* in January 1776. He argued before Congress on July 1 that it was premature to declare independence, but he persuaded few delegates. When the initial vote was taken, nine states voted for independence, with Delaware divided, New York abstaining, and South Carolina and Pennsylvania voting no. Hoping for unanimity, Congress delayed the official vote until the next day. With Caesar Rodney, after an all-night journey from Dover, breaking the tie for Delaware, and South Carolina switching its vote, only Pennsylvania and New York remained. The New York delegates were not authorized to vote on the question and again abstained. Pennsylvania potentially stood in the way of a unanimous vote for independence, but John Dickinson and Robert Morris abstained from voting, thus allowing the state's delegation to vote in favor of independence. Congress was thereby able to claim that the Declaration had passed without any colony dissenting.

As suggested earlier, Dickinson's refusal to vote for independence has hurt his reputation. His role in the Founding era has often been minimized and even distorted. At least one website erroneously claims that he was a Loyalist, and numerous scholars, following the unfair characterization of him painted by John Adams, have labeled him conservative, cautious, and timid. It is important to remember, however, that for a decade Dickinson urged resistance

> *"Dickinson's thought bears the deep impression of the Western tradition of liberal learning."*
>
> —Richard Gamble

to the first signs of British tyranny. While he preferred to maintain colonial rights within the existing empire, he also believed that preserving those rights took priority over maintaining the empire. His cautiousness was prudential, not ideological or temperamental; he thought the vote on independence ill-timed, coming before a new national government had been constructed and before any foreign aid had been secured. Until that vote, he had been the leading penman in defense of the colonists' rights.

After America's declaration of independence, Dickinson left Congress and took up his position as colonel of the First Philadelphia Battalion of Associators, a volunteer battalion that headed north to meet an expected British invasion of New York. In 1777, Dickinson, who at that time owned thirty-seven slaves and was Delaware's largest slaveholder, freed his slaves. Why he decided at this moment to manumit them is not entirely clear; however, pressure from the surrounding Quaker community (although Dickinson was not formally a Quaker, he was, as Jane Calvert has noted, deeply committed to key points of Quaker faith and practice), along with the pervasive talk of liberty and rights that filled the air, undoubtedly played a role in his decision. He returned to Congress in 1779 and in 1781 was elected president of Delaware. In October 1782 he was elected to the Supreme Executive Council of Pennsylvania (at the time, Pennsylvania had a multimember executive), and for a brief period he served as executive for both states. In 1786, Dickinson attended and was made president of the Annapolis Convention, a meeting called to "remedy defects of the federal government." Because only five states sent delegates, the convention could do little other than call for another one to be held in Philadelphia the following May.

Delaware appointed Dickinson to represent the state in the Federal Constitutional Convention of 1787. Although his attendance was interrupted by ill health, he was an active participant, and he was instrumental in laying the seed for what would later become known as the "Great," or "Connecticut," Compromise, which resolved the dispute between large and small states over representation in Congress. He also joined debates regarding the executive branch. After the Convention adjourned, Dickinson wrote nine essays urging the Constitution's ratification. These *Letters of Fabius*, which appeared in the *Delaware Gazette* beginning in early 1788 and in pamphlet form that April, were praised by Washington and other Federalists.

Dickinson began a slow process of retiring from public life after the Constitution was ratified. In 1791 he served as president of the Delaware convention called to revise that state's constitution and was one of the chief authors of the new constitution. His last notable public acts were to publish in 1797—again under the pseudonym "Fabius"—a series of fifteen letters sympathetic to France in response to what became known as the XYZ affair; then in 1803 he wrote *An Address on the Past, Present, and Eventual Relations of the United States to France* (signed "Anticipation"), which in light of Napoleon's march through Europe took a more sober view of those relations. Dickinson's primary occupation after 1788, however, was to live quietly with his wife, Mary, and two daughters in Wilmington, Delaware. In 1801 he published a two-volume collection of his writings. He died on February 14, 1808, at his Wilmington home. Upon news of his passing, Congress resolved to wear black crepe armbands in his honor, and public praise poured forth. As President Jefferson remarked, "Among the first of the advocates of the rights of his country when assailed by Great Britain, he continued to the last the orthodox advocate of the true principles of our new government."

> *"The 'penman' of the Revolution."*
>
> —Scott Douglas Gerber

Main Contributions of John Dickinson

Dickinson was the author of the important series of essays *Letters from a Farmer in Pennsylvania* (1767–1768). He has been called the "penman of the Revolution."

Dickinson was a member of the Constitutional Convention of 1787 and author of the significant Federalist essays *The Letters of Fabius* in 1788, on the Federal Constitution.

Dickinson was a delegate to the Stamp Act Congress (1765), the First and Second Continental Congresses (1774–1775), the Annapolis Convention (1786), and the Constitutional Convention (1787).

From the Pen of
John Dickinson

It is true that *impositions for raising a revenue,* may be hereafter called regulations of trade: But names will not change the nature of things. Indeed we ought firmly to believe, what is an undoubted truth, confirmed by the unhappy experience of many states heretofore free, that UNLESS THE MOST WATCHFUL ATTENTION BE EXERTED, A NEW SERVITUDE MAY BE SLIPPED UPON US, UNDER THE SANCTION OF USUAL AND RESPECTABLE TERMS.

Thus the Caesars ruined the Roman liberty, under the titles of *tribunicial and dictatorial* authorities—old and venerable dignities, known in the most flourishing times of freedom. In imitation of the same policy, James II when he meant to establish popery, *talked* of liberty of conscience, the most sacred of all liberties; and had thereby almost deceived the Dissenters into destruction.

All artful rulers, who strive to extend their power beyond its just limits, endeavor to give to their attempts as much semblance of legality as possible. Those who succeed them may venture to go a little further; for each new encroachment will be strengthened by a former. "That which is now supported by examples, growing old, will become an example itself" and thus support fresh usurpations.

A FREE people therefore can never be too quick in observing, nor too firm in opposing the beginnings of *alteration* either in *form* or *reality*, respecting institutions formed for their security. The first kind of alteration leads to the last: Yet, on the other hand, nothing is more certain, than that the *forms* of liberty may be retained, when the *substance* is gone. In government, as well as in religion, "The *letter* killeth, but the *spirit* giveth life."

—John Dickinson, Letter VI, *Letters from a Farmer in Pennsylvania*

Recommended Reading

Jane E. Calvert, *Quaker Constitutionalism and the Political Thought of John Dickinson* (New York: Cambridge University Press, 2009).

Milton E. Flower, *John Dickinson, Conservative Revolutionary* (Charlottesville: University Press of Virginia, 1983).

Forrest McDonald and Ellen S. McDonald, "John Dickinson, Founding Father," *Delaware History* 23 (1988): 24–38.

"[I]n America THE LAW IS KING."

—*Thomas Paine,* Common Sense, *1776*

"These are the times that try men's souls. The summer soldier and the sunshine Patriot will, in this crisis, shrink from the service of his country; but he that stands [by] it NOW, deserves the love and thanks of man and woman. Tyranny, like hell, is not easily conquered; yet we have this consolation with us, that the harder the conflict, the more glorious the triumph."

—*Thomas Paine,* The American Crisis, *No. 1, December 23, 1776*

"My motive and object in all my political works, beginning with Common Sense, . . . have been to rescue man from tyranny and false systems and false principles of government, and enable him to be free, and establish government for himself."

—*Thomas Paine to John Inskeep,* Philadelphia Commercial Advertiser, *February 10, 1806*

THOMAS PAINE
(1737–1809)

DAVID J. VOELKER

Thomas Paine was not the only Founder to be born outside of the thirteen colonies, but for a latecomer to America he made an astonishing impact on the Revolutionary struggle. Paine arrived in Philadelphia in late 1774 at the age of thirty-seven after suffering a variety of personal setbacks. He briefly edited a successful magazine in 1775 and then applied his talents to promoting the Revolutionary cause. His pamphlet Common Sense, *published in early 1776, championed independence and helped turn the tide of public opinion in that direction. Paine's fame in America crested during the Revolution, when he wrote a series of pamphlets to inspire the Patriot cause. His subsequent involvement in the French Revolution and vehement attacks on Christianity, however, damaged his reputation. Nevertheless, Paine deserves recognition as a Founder, not only because his pro-Revolutionary rhetoric inspired Patriots throughout the American War for Independence, but also because he helped ordinary colonists envision a prosperous American future under republican government.*

THOMAS PAINE WAS BORN INTO A FAMILY OF MODEST MEANS IN Thetford, England, a town about eighty miles from London, on January 29, 1737. Paine's mother belonged to the Church of England and saw her son baptized into this established church of the realm, but Paine was also influenced by his father's membership in the more egalitarian Society of Friends (or Quakers), a dissenting group that was merely tolerated. As a young man, Paine split the difference between his parents' churches and affiliated with Methodists, who represented a popular and evangelical offshoot of the Church of England. In the late 1750s, Paine even sometimes exhorted, or preached informally, for the Methodists.

Despite his religious upbringing, Paine eventually fell under the influence of Newtonian science, saw the universe as an orderly and mechanistic—rather than a miraculous—place. By the time he arrived in America in late 1774, Paine had already become quite impious, questioning the legitimacy of the Bible, the reality of miracles, and even the divinity of Jesus. He mostly kept his critiques of Christianity to himself at that time, however, and when he argued for the cause of independence, he drew heavily on the Bible to enrich his rhetoric. It was only in 1794, when he published a pamphlet entitled *The Age of Reason*, that Paine unleashed a vehement attack on Christianity, thus severely damaging his reputation in America. Paine's avid support of the French Revolution, which turned murderous and indeed nearly took Paine's own life, also took its toll on his popularity in America, as did his public criticism of George Washington in 1796 for endorsing the pro-British Jay Treaty.

After Paine returned to America in 1802, he suffered the humiliation of being denied the right to vote, and many of his former friends and colleagues refused to associate with him. Because he returned in the midst of a heated political battle between Republicans and Federalists, a battle in which Federalists accused the Republican leader Thomas Jefferson of being anti-Christian and Francophile, Paine became something of a persona non grata. Although Paine and his pro-republican, anticlerical writings continued to be quite influential among social critics, religious upstarts, and populist reformers, he was hardly welcomed into the pantheon of the Founding Fathers. Paine, however, deserves recognition as a Founder, not only because his pro-revolutionary rhetoric inspired Patriots throughout the American War for Independence, but also because he articulated what historian Harvey Kaye has called "the promise of America." Paine helped sell the Revolution to ordinary, free colonists by envisioning a prosperous American future under republican government.

The first thirty-seven years of Paine's life were marred by misfortune and frustration, but they also allowed Paine to begin developing talents that would serve him well later in his life. As a child, Paine attended grammar school for several years, but he spent his teenage years as an apprentice in his father's staymaking shop, where he learned to make stays for women's corsets from baleen, or whalebone. After a brief stint at sea as a privateer during the Seven Years War, Paine settled down to work as a staymaker and married Mary Lambert, but she died within a year. Paine then worked as an excise-tax officer for about three years but was fired for alleged misconduct. After working again as a staymaker and

> *"He became the great voice of revolution with publication of* Common Sense *in 1776 and rallied the Patriot cause with the series of sixteen pamphlets under the title* The American Crisis *until the end of the Revolution in 1783."*
>
> —Ellis Sandoz

then briefly as a teacher, he regained employment as a tax officer, married a woman named Elizabeth Ollive, and became active in a political debating group revealingly known as the Headstrong Club. During the winter of 1772–1773, he wrote and published his first pamphlet, in which he campaigned for higher pay for his fellow tax collectors. Because he neglected his own professional duties while lobbying in London on behalf of the excisemen, he lost his job, and his small business back home also failed. Meanwhile, his second marriage collapsed. While still in London, Paine met Benjamin Franklin, who wrote a letter of introduction for Paine and suggested that he seek his fortune across the Atlantic. Having little to lose, Paine booked passage to Philadelphia in late 1774.

Without the aid of Franklin's letter, addressed to his son-in-law in Philadelphia, Paine may well have perished. Upon his arrival in Philadelphia, Paine was so ill that he had to be carried from the ship on a litter. His fortune, however, soon improved. After he recovered, he was browsing a bookstore in Philadelphia and struck up a conversation with the store's owner, Robert Aitken. Aitken happened to be seeking an editor for the *Pennsylvania Magazine*, which he and John Witherspoon were planning to publish. Paine's program of educating himself through reading, attending lectures, and participating in debates and coffeehouse discussions paid off. He was able to show Aitken some of his writing samples and landed the job as editor.

Paine thus immersed himself in the exciting intellectual and political currents of Philadelphia in 1775. The *Philadelphia Magazine* quickly gained wide readership. He soon joined the first antislavery society in America, which was inspired in part by an antislavery essay he had published anonymously. Paine's new home of Philadelphia played an important role in the growing imperial crisis. Just before his arrival, the First Continental Congress, with delegates from twelve colonies, had met in the city. Protesting taxation without representation, the perversion of the imperial judicial system, and the treatment of Boston and Massachusetts in the wake of the Boston Tea Party, the Congress declared their rights according to their understanding

> *"For his peerless role as the pamphleteer of the American Revolution, in the course of which he transformed and extended the language of American politics, Paine deserves inclusion."*
>
> —R. B. Bernstein

of the English constitution and resolved to pressure Parliament through a nonimportation, nonconsumption, and nonexportation agreement. Tensions between the colonies and imperial government escalated into violence the following spring. On April 19, 1775, fighting broke out between the "minutemen" of Lexington and Concord (in Massachusetts), and the British soldiers who had marched out of Boston in search of colonial stockpiles of arms and ammunition. By May 10, the Second Continental Congress convened in Philadelphia, and a month later the Congress created a Continental Army to be led by George Washington.

Although Paine did not yet jump directly into the political fray, the February 1775 issue of his magazine included an essay critical of the colonial consumption of British tea. By July the magazine published two allegorical essays that championed the right of the colonists to defend their liberty and property from British aggression. More strikingly, the magazine reprinted the Second Continental Congress's strident "Declaration . . . Setting Forth the Causes and Necessity of Their Taking Up Arms," which reached a powerful conclusion:

In our own native land, in defence of the freedom that is our birthright, and which we ever enjoyed till the late violation of it—for the protection of our property, acquired solely by the honest industry of our fore-fathers and ourselves, against violence actually offered, we have taken up arms. We shall lay them down when hostilities shall cease on the part of the aggressors, and all danger of their being renewed shall be removed, and not before.

Paine's magazine thus signaled that it came down squarely on the side of the aggrieved colonists.

By the fall of 1775, Paine had concluded that the American colonies needed to unite behind the cause of independence. He had also reached the end of his partnership with Aitken and Witherspoon; he resigned his editorship because of disagreements over his salary. His break from the magazine, however, freed him to compose a pamphlet in support of independence—a project that he had been discussing with Philadelphia physician Benjamin Rush (another neglected Founder).

Published anonymously in January 1776, Paine's *Common Sense* became the most widely read pamphlet in eighteenth century America (by far). Hundreds of thousands of colonists either read the pamphlet themselves or heard it read aloud and discussed. Drawing on history, biblical examples, and what he called "common sense," Paine took a novel approach to arguing for independence. Most of his fellow Patriots had long admired the English constitution. Indeed, the various protest documents issued by the colonists appealed to the English constitution—which was a political and legal tradition rather than a single written document—as the source of their liberties. Paine, by contrast, directly attacked the constitution by condemning the monarchy and aristocracy. He even attacked the structure of English society itself as fundamentally dysfunctional. Furthermore, he pointed out the absurdity of an island governing the continent of North America indefinitely. He also dramatized the importance of the Patriot cause in memorable language: "The sun never shined on a cause of greater worth. 'Tis not the affair of a city, a country, a province, or a kingdom, but of a continent. . . . 'Tis not the concern of a day, a year, or an age; posterity are virtually involved in the contest, and will be more or less affected, even until the end of time. Now is the seed time of continental union, faith, and honor."

Common Sense went even further to make the case for independence. First, Paine addressed the pamphlet to ordinary Americans, making it clear that they had a stake in the future status of their provinces. He accomplished this end in part by writing in accessible and vivid prose, with frequent allusions to the well-known Protestant Bible. Paine also used his political imagination to project an image of a democratic republic. Visualizing a primordial political assembly, for example, Paine wrote: "Some convenient tree will afford them a State-House, under the branches of which, the whole colony may assemble to deliberate on public matters." He also made suggestions about the future government of the "United Colonies." Here, he boldly recommended that the colonies hold a conference to frame a "CONTINENTAL CHARTER," which amounted to nothing less than a written constitution. In sum, Paine sketched a powerful image of a republican society, a society where all citizens would be equal, where the law would be king, and where Americans of all origins and faiths could pursue prosperity in peace.

Historians agree that Paine's *Common Sense* helped convince colonists that the time had indeed come for declaring independence, but it is also worth noting Paine's contribution to the concept of American exceptionalism—the belief that America offered unique opportunities for freedom and prosperity and that the American people had a special duty to strive to fulfill this destiny. Near the conclusion of *Common Sense*, for example, Paine declared: "We have it in our power to begin the world over again. A situation, similar to the present, hath not happened since the days of Noah until now. The birthday of a new world is at hand, and a race of men, perhaps as numerous as all Europe contains, are to receive their portion of freedom from the event of a few months." Although Paine later repudiated any belief in special providence (God's direct intervention in human affairs), his *American Crisis* pamphlet series brimmed with references to God favoring the Patriot cause. At the close of the January 13, 1777, *Crisis*, for instance, Paine predicted: "Our independence, with God's blessing, we will maintain against all the world." In all of his Revolutionary writings, Paine conveyed the notion that God supported American liberation, and "Americans"—a label that Paine promoted—had an obligation to seize the opportunity. In *The Last Crisis* of April 19, 1783, Paine reiterated the Revolution's significance: "To see it in our power to make a world happy—to teach mankind the art of being so—to exhibit on the theatre of the universe a character hitherto unknown—and to have, as it were, a new creation entrusted to our hands, are honors that command reflection, and can neither be too highly estimated, nor too gratefully received." With this sort of rhetoric, Paine contributed to Americans' sense that their especially blessed nation had a unique mission to promote liberty.

Paine gave his most important service to the Revolutionary cause as a pamphleteer, with all royalties for his publications going to support the war effort, but he also filled various official posts during the war. In the summer of 1776, Paine enlisted in a militia unit as secretary to General Daniel Roberdeau; when that term ended in the fall of 1776, he enlisted in the Continental Army, where he served as an aide to General Nathanael Greene. Between 1777 and 1779, Paine worked as secretary to the Continental Congress's Committee on Foreign Affairs. Meanwhile, he promoted the unusually democratic constitution of Pennsylvania, whose framers had been deeply influenced by the constitutional plan that he had laid out in *Common Sense*. From 1779 to 1781 he served as the clerk for Pennsylvania's legislative assembly. In 1781 he traveled to France to solicit wartime assistance, and he even participated in combat during the journey. Unfortunately for his livelihood, Paine also made a number of political enemies by (legitimately) attacking Silas Deane, an American agent to France, with charges of corruption. As the Revolution came to a close, Paine found himself unemployed, but by 1785 he had garnered modest grants of money and land from Pennsylvania, New York, and Congress.

After the war, Paine continued to write on political issues important to establishing national unity, but he turned his attention to another type of project, namely promoting his design for an iron bridge capable of spanning long distances. Although he pursued this project for several years and made significant engineering advancements, his quests to secure funding in the U.S., Britain, and France all fell short, and he never fully implemented his design.

By 1789 international developments redirected Paine's energies back toward revolutionary politics. That summer, a popular uprising in France led to the overthrow of the feudal order and the establishment, initially, of a constitutional monarchy. When British conservative Edmund Burke decried the revolutionary disorder in a widely read treatise of 1790, Paine responded with a two-part pamphlet entitled *Rights of Man* (1791–1792). For an eighteenth-century political pamphlet, the popularity of *Rights of Man* was second only to *Common Sense*, but its influence spread even broader, as it was read not only in the U.S. and Britain but also in France and elsewhere in Europe. *Rights of Man* reaffirmed and elaborated upon the political principles that Paine had first sketched out in *Common Sense*, especially the "equality of man" and the right to self-government. Because the tract threatened monarchical authority, Paine was convicted in Britain in absentia of seditious libel; his writings were banned in Britain, and he was effectively exiled.

Paine narrowly escaped arrest in Britain in September 1792 by fleeing to France, where he had been awarded honorary citizenship and a seat in the National Convention. He did not speak fluent French, but he was appointed to a committee charged with drafting a constitution. Despite his prominent position, Paine soon found himself in serious jeopardy. As two factions struggled for control over the revolutionary government, Paine sided with the moderate Girondins by (unsuccessfully) opposing the execution of King Louis XVI. When the radical Jacobins, led by Maximilian Robespierre, seized power in 1793, they began arresting and executing their political enemies. Along with other foreigners, Paine found himself ejected from the Convention in December 1793 and imprisoned. While in prison for nearly a year, Paine suffered from ill health and narrowly escaped execution. Thanks to the advocacy of James Monroe, the American ambassador to France, Paine was released from prison in late 1794 and was restored to his position in the Convention, where he continued to serve through the following year.

Just before he was imprisoned, Paine completed the manuscript for the first part of *The Age of Reason: Being an Investigation of True and of Fabulous Theology*, which was published in the U.S. in two parts in 1794 and 1795 and was also translated into French. Paine

wrote *The Age of Reason* in part to respond to the political emer-
gency that threatened his own life. As he later explained in a public
letter to Samuel Adams (who was deeply offended by the book),
"My friends were falling as fast as the guillotine could cut their
heads off," and "the people of France were running headlong into
Atheism." Although most Americans perceived *The Age of Reason*
primarily as a scurrilous attack on Christianity in particular and
revealed religion in general, Paine also wrote to promote a deistic
morality that he believed would prevent atrocities like the Jacobin
Terror.

Nevertheless, he devoted most of the work to condemning
Christianity. "The Christian theory," he wrote, "is little else than
the idolatry of the ancient mythologists, accommodated to the
purposes of power and revenue." Paine expressed equally harsh
views of the Bible: "When I see throughout the greatest part of
this book, scarcely any thing but a history of the grossest vices,
and a collection of the most paltry and contemptible tales, I cannot dishonour my Creator by calling it by his name." As for Jesus,
Paine believed that "[h]e was a virtuous and an amiable man" who
preached a "benevolent" morality that "has not been exceeded by
any." Not surprisingly, however, Paine rejected and condemned
the supernatural aura surrounding Jesus, whom he considered to
be merely human. Paine rejected the Christian virtue of loving
one's enemy, as he found it impracticable, but he suggested that
the moral implications of the "book of Creation" were clear: "The
Almighty lecturer, by displaying the principles of science in the
structure of the universe, has invited man to study and to imitation. It is as if he had said to the inhabitants of this globe that
we call ours, 'I have made an earth for man to dwell upon, and
I have rendered the starry heavens visible, to teach him science
and the arts. He can now provide for his own comfort, AND

LEARN FROM MY MUNIFICENCE TO ALL, TO BE KIND TO EACH OTHER.'" Creation, according to Paine, enjoined humanity to follow the golden rule.

The Age of Reason went through an impressive twenty-one American reprints within a decade. But the denunciations came quickly as well. Within fifteen years, the book had been met with almost seventy responses in America and England. Several years later, in 1802, after Paine became disillusioned with Napoleon and left France for America, he found that his reputation there had been severely tarnished. To be sure, some of his old friends welcomed him heartily, as did substantial numbers of the Democratic-Republicans. He maintained friendships with Thomas Jefferson (who helped him return to America), James Monroe (who had helped secure his release from prison in France), and James Madison. Many of his associates from the Revolutionary period, however, turned their backs on Paine. John Adams (who had long mistrusted Paine), Samuel Adams, Benjamin Rush, John Jay, Patrick Henry, and Elias Boudinot all reacted very negatively to Paine's attacks on Christianity.

Nevertheless, Paine was by no means forgotten after his death in 1809. On the contrary, as Harvey J. Kaye has argued in *Thomas Paine and the Promise of America*, Paine's writings inspired not only deists and other religious outsiders but also a wide variety of democratic reformers and freethinkers.

Paine's legacy lived on, as nineteenth-century Americans continued to spread the influence of republican principles and to expand the nation he helped create.

Main Contributions of Thomas Paine

Paine's pamphlet *Common Sense* played a crucial role in persuading Americans that the time had come to declare independence from Britain. Crucially, the pamphlet envisioned a prosperous future for an egalitarian and self-governed America.

Paine's pamphlet series *The American Crisis* helped sustain Patriotism throughout the Revolutionary War.

Paine's writings promoted a republican and democratic spirit that inspired generations of American activists and reformers.

From the Pen of Thomas Paine

The cause of America is in a great measure the cause of all mankind. Many circumstances hath, and will arise, which are not local, but universal, and through which the principles of all Lovers of Mankind are affected, and in the Event of which, their Affections are interested. The laying of a Country desolate with Fire and Sword, declaring War against the natural rights of all Mankind, and extirpating the Defenders thereof from the Face of the Earth, is the Concern of every Man to whom Nature hath given the Power of feeling. . . .

A government of our own is our natural right: And when a man seriously reflects on the precariousness of human affairs, he will become convinced, that it is infinitely wiser and safer, to form a constitution of our own in a cool deliberate manner, while we have it in our power, than to trust such an interesting event to time and chance.

O ye that love mankind! Ye that dare oppose, not only the tyranny, but the tyrant, stand forth! Every spot of the old world is overrun with oppression. Freedom hath been hunted round the globe. Asia, and Africa, have long expelled her.—Europe regards her like a stranger, and England hath given her warning to depart. O! receive the fugitive, and prepare in time an asylum for mankind.

—Thomas Paine, *Common Sense* (1776)

Recommended Reading

Michael Foot and Isaac Kramnick, ed. *The Thomas Paine Reader* (New York: Penguin, 1987).

Harvey J. Kaye, *Thomas Paine and the Promise of America* (New York: Hill and Wang, 2005).

John Keane, *Tom Paine: A Political Life* (New York: Grove Press, 2003).

David J. Voelker, "Thomas Paine's Civil Religion of Reason," in *The Forgotten Founders on Religion and Public Life*, ed. Daniel L. Dreisbach, Mark David Hall, and Jeffry H. Morrison (Notre Dame: University of Notre Dame Press, 2009), 171–95.

"I have but one lamp by which my feet are guided, and that is the lamp of experience. I know of no way of judging of the future but by the past."

—*Patrick Henry, "Liberty or Death" Speech, 1775*

"This Constitution is said to have beautiful features; but when I come to examine these features, Sir, they appear to me horridly frightful: Among other deformities, it has an awful squinting; it squints towards monarchy."

—*Patrick Henry, Speech at Virginia Ratifying Convention, 1788*

PATRICK HENRY
(1736–1799)

THOMAS S. KIDD

Patrick Henry was one of the most influential Patriots who promoted resistance to British authority during the American Revolution. In 1765, as a freshman member of Virginia's colonial legislature, Henry introduced the Stamp Act Resolutions and gave a fiery speech against King George III that elicited cries of treason from other legislators. Henry served in the First and Second Continental Congresses, but his most famous speech came at the Virginia Convention in March 1775, where he famously declared "Give me liberty or give me death!" The popular Henry led a militia to recover gunpowder seized by Virginia's royal governor in April 1775. Once independence was proclaimed, Henry served as Virginia's first governor from 1776 to 1779, an office he held again from 1784 to 1786. During the 1780s, Henry disagreed with his fellow Revolutionary leaders James Madison and Thomas Jefferson over a number of issues, including the role of religion in Virginia society. While Madison successfully pushed through Jefferson's Bill for Estab-

*lishing Religious Freedom in 1786, Henry advocated contin-
ued state support for Christian ministers. Henry also opposed
Madison's new Federal Constitution in 1787–1788, and Henry
became one of America's leading Anti-Federalists. He eventually became supportive of the new federal government and
remained especially close with George Washington.*

PATRICK HENRY WAS BORN ON MAY 29, 1736, TO JOHN AND SARAH
Henry of Hanover County, Virginia. Henry's family did not belong
to the old Virginia aristocracy, but they were up-and-coming residents of central Virginia. Henry only briefly attended grammar
school, and did not go to college. Nevertheless, he received significant training from his father in essential topics of the liberal arts,
especially ancient and modern history.

Henry married his first wife, Sarah, in 1754, and twice as a
young man he launched small stores that went bankrupt. He
briefly worked as a barkeeper at his father-in-law's tavern, where he
first met Thomas Jefferson in 1759. There had been little indication
of Henry's coming rise to prominence when he finally acquired his
law license in 1760.

One of the formative influences on Henry as a youth was the
new evangelical faith emerging from the First Great Awakening that started in the 1740s. Virginia maintained state support
for the Anglican church (Church of England), so the emotional
preaching style of the upstart Presbyterians and Baptists was not
welcomed by many Virginians. But Henry's mother came under
the influence of Hanover's famous Presbyterian pastor Samuel
Davies, whose compelling sermons won her over. She report-
edly took young Patrick to Davies's meetings in the 1740s, and
Henry remembered Davies as the "greatest orator he ever heard."
Although Henry remained an Anglican, he adapted the evan-

gelical preaching style to his political speeches, with explosive results.

Religious issues also gave Henry his first opportunity to confront the problem of royal authority in America in a case that became known as the Parson's Cause. Virginia reduced Anglican priests' salaries under the Two Penny Act of 1758, but the British Privy Council, with approval from the king, overturned the law. Henry defended Louisa County, Virginia, in a lawsuit brought by one of the priests to recover lost salary. Henry turned the case into an attack on British power in the colonies, exclaiming that "a King, by annulling or disallowing Laws of this salutary Nature, from being the Father of his People, degenerates into a Tyrant, and forfeits all Right to his Subjects' Obedience." Having tapped into popular resentment

> *"Like many Americans over the course of the rest of American history, Henry believed that our inalienable rights were best protected by strong and vigorous state and local governments."*
>
> —Stephen B. Presser

against Britain, Henry convinced the jury to insult the priest further by awarding only one penny in damages.

Henry's growing popularity led to his election to the Virginia House of Burgesses, the colonial legislature, in 1765. His arrival in the House coincided with the coming of the Stamp Act crisis, during which many Americans began to protest the imposition of taxes by Parliament. Henry immediately seized the spotlight by introducing resolutions against the Stamp Act, helping Americans articulate their belief that they should be taxed only by their own elected legislatures, not Parliament.

In his speech defending the resolutions, Henry again challenged not only Parliament's power but also, most provocatively, the king's. A visitor to the House reported that Henry proclaimed that "in former times Tarquin and Jul[i]us had their Brutus, Charles had his Cromwell, and he did not doubt but some good American would stand up, in favour of his Country." The implication seemed clear—Henry was warning that King George III might be assassinated if he became tyrannical. Understandably, the speech drew a rebuke from the Speaker, who declared that Henry had spoken treason. Henry backed down, but he had made his point. The resolutions electrified the colonies, giving a focal point to the growing resistance movement.

Henry moved in and out of the spotlight in the Revolutionary crisis, as he continued to spend a great deal of time on private business and legal affairs. But in 1774, as the tension between Britain and the colonies entered its most acute phase, Virginians chose him to serve along with George Washington and others in the First Continental Congress in Philadelphia. One of Henry's greatest moments in the Congress came when he proclaimed that "the distinctions between Virginians, Pennsylvanians, New Yorkers, and New Englanders, are no more. I am not a Virginian, but an American." Intercolonial cooperation was nearly unprecedented but was badly needed in light of the coming struggle. Henry, with other radicals such as John and Samuel Adams, prevented the Congress from offering conciliatory measures and helped steer America toward war.

Back in Virginia, Henry's support for defensive measures against Britain led him to give his most celebrated oration, the "Liberty or Death" speech. While some Virginians hesitated at the prospect of armed conflict, Henry demanded that the time for war had come: "We must fight! I repeat it, sir, we must fight! An appeal to arms and to the God of hosts, is all that is left us! . . . Is life so dear, or peace so sweet, as to be purchased at the price of chains and slavery? Forbid it, Almighty God!" With this, Henry lifted his arms and cried, "I know not what course others may take; but as for me, give me liberty, or give me death!" The exhilarated Virginia Convention adopted Henry's plan for defending itself against Britain.

Soon after the "Liberty or Death" speech, Virginia's royal governor, Lord Dunmore, decided to seize the colonists' gunpowder held at Williamsburg. Henry, becoming as much a military leader as a politician, led a volunteer militia company from Hanover County to retake the gunpowder. Cooler heads prevailed, and Henry accepted a promise of compensation for the gunpowder from the governor's agents. The angry Dunmore still declared Henry an outlaw, however. Henry's persistent radicalism helped set the stage for Virginia, and America, to declare independence in 1776.

Henry was an obvious choice as Virginia's first governor, an office he held from 1776 to 1779, and again from 1784 to 1786. In 1777, Henry married his second wife, Dorothea, following the death of his first wife in 1775. Altogether, Henry had seventeen children.

During the 1780s, Henry developed a bitter rivalry with his former Patriot brethren Thomas Jefferson and James Madison. Jefferson, working as an ambassador in Paris, became so disgusted with the feud that he once wrote Madison that they should pray for Henry to die. One of the sharpest points of contention between them was state support for religion in Virginia. Tax support for the Anglican Church had been suspended in 1776, but many Virginians, including Henry and George Washington, still believed that a moral society needed government support for religion. In 1784, Henry introduced a measure for a "general assessment" for religion, under which residents could designate the church to receive their taxes. But when Henry left the legislature to return to the governor's mansion, Madison seized the opportunity to defeat Henry's plan. A flood of petitions from non-Episcopal evangelicals opposed the general assessment. Riding the wave of popular sentiment, Madison managed to pass Jefferson's Bill for Establishing Religious Freedom in 1786. This act banned tax support for religion and prohibited legal penalties for unorthodox beliefs.

Henry also opposed Madison's new Constitution for the United States, adopted at the Constitutional Convention in 1787. Henry became one of America's most influential Anti-Federalists, arguing that the proposed Constitution threatened the states with unchecked national power. Henry's opposition to the Constitution may be difficult to understand today, but he represented a number of prominent Patriot leaders who had serious misgivings about the proposed new government. As legal historian Stephen B. Presser has noted, "Like many Americans over the course of the rest of American history, Henry believed that our inalienable rights were best protected by strong and vigorous state and local governments." He could not stomach the vast new powers afforded to the national government.

> *"Henry's powerful oratory was instrumental in marshalling Americans to the cause of independence in the early to mid-1770s. In the late 1780s, he emerged as a leading Anti-Federalist, and his opposition to the proposed national Constitution of 1787 was responsible, in part, for the debate over amendments to the Constitution, which resulted in the adoption of the U.S. Bill of Rights."*
>
> —Daniel L. Dreisbach

At the Virginia ratifying convention, Henry nearly convinced delegates to reject the Constitution, warning that it represented "a revolution as radical as that which separated us from Great Britain. . . . The rights of conscience, trial by jury, liberty of the press, all your immunities and franchises, all pretensions to human rights and privileges, are rendered insecure, if not lost, by this change." The adoption of the Bill of Rights by the first Congress helped alleviate some of these fears, and Henry quickly reconciled with the new government.

By the 1790s, Henry had seemingly switched roles with Jefferson and Madison, as he became affiliated with Washington's Federalist Party and at times defended stronger national power. After declining several federal positions, including secretary of state in 1795, Henry was again elected to Virginia's legislature in 1799. He died that year before taking office.

Henry was greatly admired by other Revolutionary leaders, primarily for his courage and oratorical brilliance. Silas Deane of Connecticut wrote that Henry was the "compleatest speaker I ever heard . . . but in a letter I can give you no idea of the music of his voice, or the highwrought yet natural elegance of his style and manner." George Mason of Virginia wrote that Henry was "by far the most powerful speaker I ever heard. Every word he says not only engages but commands the attention; and your passions are no longer your own when he addresses them. But his eloquence is the smallest part of his merit. He is in my opinion the first man upon this continent, as well in abilities as public virtues, and had he lived in Rome about the time of the first Punic War, when the Roman people had arrived at their meridian glory, and their virtue not tarnished, Mr. Henry's talents must have put him at the head of that glorious commonwealth."

Main Contributions of Patrick Henry

In 1765, Henry introduced Virginia's resolutions against the Stamp Act, which focused resistance against the act in the colonies.

In 1775, Henry delivered his "Liberty or Death" speech at the Virginia Convention, which galvanized Virginia's commitment to fight against Britain.

During the debates over ratification of the U.S. Constitution of 1787, Henry became one of America's leading Anti-Federalists, fearing that the Constitution represented a dangerous seizure of power by the national government.

From the Pen of
Patrick Henry

Let us not, I beseech you, sir, deceive ourselves. Sir, we have done everything that could be done to avert the storm which is now coming on. We have petitioned; we have remonstrated; we have supplicated; we have prostrated ourselves before the throne, and have implored its interposition to arrest the tyrannical hands of the ministry and Parliament. Our petitions have been slighted; our remonstrances have produced additional violence and insult; our supplications have been disregarded; and we have been spurned, with contempt, from the foot of the throne! In vain, after these things, may we indulge the fond hope of peace and reconciliation. There is no longer any room for hope. If we wish to be free—if we mean to preserve inviolate those inestimable privileges for which we have been so long contending—if we mean not basely to abandon the noble struggle in which we have been so long engaged, and which we have pledged ourselves never to abandon until the glorious object of our contest shall be obtained—we must fight! I repeat it, sir, we must fight! An appeal to arms and to the God of hosts is all that is left us!

They tell us, sir, that we are weak; unable to cope with so formidable an adversary. But when shall we be stronger? Will it be the next week, or the next year? Will it be when we are totally disarmed, and when a British guard shall be stationed in every house? Shall we gather strength by irresolution and inaction? Shall we acquire the means of effectual resistance by lying supinely on our backs and hugging the delusive phantom of hope, until our enemies shall have bound us hand and foot? Sir, we are not weak if we make a proper use of those means which the God of nature hath placed in our power. The millions of people, armed in the holy cause of liberty, and in such a country as that which we possess, are invincible by any force which our enemy can send against us. Besides, sir, we shall not fight our battles alone. There is a just God who presides over the destinies of nations, and who will raise up friends to fight our battles for us. The battle, sir, is not to the strong alone; it is to the vigilant, the active, the brave. Besides, sir, we have no election. If we were base enough to desire it, it is now too late to retire from the contest. There is no retreat but in submission and slavery! Our chains are forged! Their clanking may be heard on the plains of Boston! The war is inevitable—and let it come! I repeat it, sir, let it come.

It is in vain, sir, to extenuate the matter. Gentlemen may cry, Peace, Peace—but there is no peace. The war is actually begun! The next gale that sweeps from the north will bring to our ears the clash of resounding arms! Our brethren are already in the field! Why stand we here idle? What is it that gentlemen wish? What would they have? Is life so dear, or peace so sweet, as to be purchased at the price of chains and slavery? Forbid it, Almighty God! I know not what course others may take; but as for me, give me liberty or give me death!

—Patrick Henry, "Liberty or Death" Speech (1775)

Recommended Reading

Richard R. Beeman, *Patrick Henry: A Biography* (New York: McGraw-Hill, 1974).

William Wirt Henry, *Patrick Henry: Life, Correspondence, and Speeches*, 3 vols. (New York: Charles Scribner's Sons, 1891).

Henry Mayer, *A Son of Thunder: Patrick Henry and the American Republic* (New York: F. Watts, 1986).

Thomas S. Kidd, *Patrick Henry: First among Patriots* (New York: Basic Books, 2011).

"There is not a single instance in history, in which civil liberty was lost, and religious liberty preserved entire. If therefore we yield up our temporal property, we at the same time deliver the conscience into bondage."

> —*John Witherspoon, "The Dominion of Providence over the Passions of Men," 1776*

"[T]he practice of true and undefiled religion . . . is the great foundation of public prosperity and national happiness."

> —*John Witherspoon, Congressional Thanksgiving Day Proclamation, 1782*

"[C]ivil liberty cannot be long preserved without virtue."

> —*John Witherspoon, "Sermon at a Public Thanksgiving," 1782*

JOHN WITHERSPOON
(1723–1794)

JEFFRY H. MORRISON

In 1774, John Adams, who had no patience for fools or preachers, called the Reverend John Witherspoon of Princeton a "clear, sensible" clergyman and "as high a Son of Liberty, as any Man in America." Witherspoon's Revolutionary activities between 1776 and 1783 would validate Adams's assessment. He served on New Jersey's committee of correspondence and was the first man in that colony to call for independence from Great Britain. Witherspoon was appointed to the Second Continental Congress in late June 1776. He arrived in time to urge independence for the united colonies, and he was the only active clergyman to sign the Declaration of Independence. Indeed, he was the most influential political parson during America's Founding period. He was possibly the most active member of the Second Continental Congress during the Revolution and was president of the College of New Jersey at Princeton during one of the most important quarter centuries (1768–1794) in the whole of American history. In Explaining America, *Garry*

Wills noted that he was "probably the most influential teacher in the entire history of American education." In each of these roles—preacher, Patriot, college president—Witherspoon was outstanding. Writing more than a decade after Witherspoon's death, his old friend Benjamin Rush mused, "He was a man of a great and luminous mind. . . . His works will probably preserve his name to the end of time." His reputation continued high through the nineteenth century, but by the early twentieth century, the public began to forget the works and name of the parson-politician from New Jersey.

JOHN WITHERSPOON, D.D., LL.D., LIVED A REMARKABLE LIFE THAT spanned the last three quarters of the eighteenth century. Born the same year as Adam Smith, at the dawn of the Scottish Enlightenment, he was educated at its heart at the University of Edinburgh. At the urging of Benjamin Rush, the trustees of the College of New Jersey at Princeton, and George Whitefield, the Anglican evangelist who helped touch off the First

> *"Remarkable teacher of James Madison and a generation of mid-Atlantic elites who went to the college of New Jersey (Princeton) and made revolutionary republican ideals respectable."*
>
> —David J. Siemers

Great Awakening, Witherspoon immigrated to Princeton in 1768 to become the sixth president of the college. He remained there during the crucial Founding years of the Republic until his death in 1794. Witherspoon's political career was spent at the Founding's epicenter—in and around Philadelphia during its crisis years. He served periodically in the New Jersey provincial and state legislatures (1774–1789), in the Continental and Confederation Congresses throughout the Revolution (1776–1782), and in the New Jersey convention that ratified the federal Constitution (1787). In signing the Declaration of Independence and the Articles of Confederation, and in ratifying the Constitution, Witherspoon had a direct hand in passing three of the four organic laws of the United States.

John Witherspoon had three careers, any one of which should have guaranteed him a prominent and lasting place in American history. As pastor, college president, and politician, his various careers combined in interesting ways. He was the only active clergyman and college president to sign the Declaration of Independence, which secured him a place that is literally unique among the Founders, at the crossroads of religion, education, and politics. Witherspoon was also an amateur scientist, political economist, rhetorician, and philosopher; in short, he was a polymath. His interests and abilities made him the sort of well-rounded man we associate with American Enlightenment characters like Thomas Jefferson and Benjamin Franklin. Like those two, Witherspoon was an intellectual handyman with a scientific bent; for instance, he was elected an officer in Franklin's American Philosophical Society the same year as Jefferson and the astronomer David Rittenhouse. But unlike those colleagues in the society, Witherspoon added the roles of theologian and moral philosopher to his scientific and political interests.

By the summer of 1776, when he led the New Jersey delegation to the Second Continental Congress in Philadelphia, Witherspoon had already been active in provincial politics for several years. He had been on the Committee of Correspondence from Somerset County since its inception and had been a delegate to the New Jersey Provincial Congress from 1774 until his appointment to the Continental Congress in June 1776. His record in the Congress reveals that, excepting part of the year 1780, Witherspoon was scrupulous in his attendance and almost preternaturally active. *The*

Journals of the Continental Congress record Witherspoon's appointment to 126 committees in his six years of service, including two crucial "standing" or permanent committees, the Committee on Foreign Affairs and the Board of War. Witherspoon got the attention of his congressional colleagues early and held it throughout the next six years. Sometime during the debates on July 1 and 2, 1776, a member of the conservative faction (probably John Dickinson of Pennsylvania) argued that the country at large was not yet ripe for independence. Witherspoon promptly responded that, in his judgment, the colonies were not only ripe for independence but also "in danger of becoming rotten for the want of it." By so replying, he helped prod Congress toward passing Richard Henry Lee's Resolution for Independence on July 2, and the Declaration of Independence two days later. Appointment to a prodigious number of committees followed immediately and did not abate until Witherspoon retired from Congress at the end of 1782. It is a further measure of the confidence other congressmen placed in him that Witherspoon was tapped to draw up the instructions to the American peace commission in France in 1781.

Witherspoon also made less formal, though no less important, contributions to the Founding. He preached a number of politically influential sermons and was a productive pamphleteer, especially during the Revolutionary period. Several of his political pamphlets and speeches have been preserved in his *Works*, including: "Reflections on the Present State of Public Affairs"; "On Conducting the American Controversy"; "On the Contest Between Great Britain and America"; "On the Affairs of the United States"; a piece on Thomas Paine's *Common Sense* over the pseudonym "Aristides"; and a series of periodical essays that he signed "the Druid."

Nor did Witherspoon's political influence end with his retirement from politics in 1789. The list of his Princeton graduates reads like a roll of early American notables. Among these were twelve members of the Continental Congress, five delegates to the Constitutional Convention, one U.S. president (James Madison), a vice president (Aaron Burr), seventy-seven U.S. congressmen, three Supreme Court justices, eight U.S. district court judges, one secretary of state, three attorneys general, and two foreign ministers. In addition to these national office holders, twenty-six of Witherspoon's graduates were state judges, seventeen were members of their state constitutional conventions, and fourteen were delegates to the state conventions that ratified the Constitution. Chief among Witherspoon's graduates was, of course, James Madison, Father of the Constitution and reluctant architect of the Bill of Rights. Madison stayed on an extra term following his graduation to study Hebrew and the law under the "Old Doctor's" direction and then proceeded to carry certain elements of Witherspoon's political-theological creed into his own public career, culminating in two stormy terms as president from 1809 to 1817.

So intertwined were Witherspoon's political and pastoral careers, not to mention his political theory and his theology, that his political career cannot adequately be appreciated without understanding his status as a clergyman. Witherspoon came from a long and distinguished line of Reformed (i.e., Calvinist) pastors, and his mother claimed lineal descent from the Scottish Reformer John Knox. In Britain and Europe, he had gained fame as the outspoken leader of the democratic and evangelical Popular Party that opposed the more traditional (though theologically liberal) Moderate Party of Francis Hutcheson in the Scottish Presbyterian church, and as the author of two widely cited satirical pieces written during his Scottish ministry. Thus, by the time he received the call to Princeton in 1768, Witherspoon was already something of an international figure in ecclesiastical circles.

His reputation continued to rise in America. He quickly formed powerful connections throughout the colonies, from fellow pastors like Ezra Stiles and Timothy Dwight in New England, to family—one of his daughters married Madison's friend the Reverend Samuel Stanhope Smith, who founded what became Hampden-Sydney College in Virginia and years later succeeded Witherspoon as president of Princeton—and Presbyterian colleagues in the Carolinas and Georgia. Doctor Witherspoon was a fixture in the joint conventions the Presbyterians had with the Congregationalists of the General Association of Connecticut. These conventions were originally convened to ally the two denominations against a potential Anglican establishment, that perennial bugaboo of dissenting colonial Protestants. There his lifelong friendship with the Reverend Ezra Stiles, the president of Yale College who found Witherspoon "a very learned divine" but complained privately that he was too much of a politician, was strengthened.

From 1785 through 1789, Reverend Witherspoon was the leading figure in nationalizing the American Presbyterian Church. Out of that nationalization came catechisms, a confession, a directory of worship, and an ecclesiastical constitution called "the Form of the Government," of which portions were written by Witherspoon. His introduction to the Form of the Government set out the first principles of church polity for the new national church. Due primarily to his influence, the Form of the Government contained articles that strongly upheld religious liberty and in fact liberalized the Westminster Confession of Faith of 1647.

His denominational and national prominence gave Witherspoon's sermons, many of which were printed and circulated extensively, considerable weight. Weightiest of all was his first explicitly political sermon, "The Dominion of Providence over the Passions of Men," preached on May 17, 1776, a congressional fast day. The first edition of "The Dominion of Providence" was printed that year by Robert Aitken of Philadelphia, whose congressionally approved edition of the Bible would later become the first English Bible printed in North America. Second and third editions of the sermon were reprinted in Glasgow in 1777, accompanied by annotations in which Witherspoon was called a rebel and a traitor; a fourth was reprinted in Philadelphia and London in 1777, and a fifth was brought out in London in 1779. The overwhelmingly favorable American response to the sermon helped rally support for independence, especially in New Jersey, which was not keen on independence just then, and vaulted Witherspoon into the Continental Congress in late June of 1776. As the de facto head of the New Jersey delegation in Congress, and of all colonial Presbyterians, Witherspoon was ideally positioned to spur the independence movement forward.

In addition to "The Dominion of Providence" and his other political sermons, Witherspoon was the author of one congressional fast day proclamation and two thanksgiving day proclamations, fully a third of Congress's religious proclamations during the years he was a member of that body. These proclamations are quintessential examples of the theological-political ethos of the Revolutionary years. Many of their themes—the Almighty's providential care for the United States, the necessity of religion and morality for civic health— were the stock-in-trade of late-eighteenth-century-American political orations such as Washington's Farewell Address. Witherspoon incorporated those

"He was a real workhorse in the Revolutionary cause as well as a teacher to many of the new nation's principal leaders, including James Madison. As a Founding Father, he plays second fiddle to none!"

—Thomas Buckley

proclamation themes into his sermons and lectures to upperclass-men and divinity students.

In addition to his duties as president of the College of New Jer-sey, Witherspoon taught the capstone course on moral philosophy to graduating seniors, as well as courses on rhetoric, history, and divinity. It is commonly acknowledged that the "Lectures on Elo-quence," first given as class lectures by President Witherspoon and later published in his *Works* beginning in 1800–1801, were "the first American rhetorical treatise." In fact, Witherspoon was responsible for a number of firsts in America. He published a series of essays from 1776 to 1781 under the pseudonym "the Druid" in which he included observations on the American language and even coined the word *Americanism*. Witherspoon has also been attributed with introducing the Latin word *campus* into the American lexicon when he used it to describe the grounds at Princeton in 1774. But President Witherspoon's *Lectures on Moral Philosophy* marked a critical first in American higher education: a systematic treatment of moral philosophy, which was then coming into vogue in the colonial colleges. Derived largely, though not slavishly, from Fran-cis Hutcheson's *System of Moral Philosophy* (1755), these lectures of Witherspoon's—in oral, manuscript, and published forms—were vastly influential. Manuscripts of the lectures, which were copied verbatim from a syllabus by each member of the senior class at Princeton for a quarter century, circulated widely throughout the colonies. In 1820 the University of Pennsylvania was still listing "Witherspoon," along with "Hutcheson, Paley [and] Smith," as a text on "natural and political law."

Throughout the Revolution, Witherspoon had continually traveled between Princeton and Philadelphia, teaching and presid-ing over the college, preaching and ministering in the local Pres-byterian church and in the synod of New York and Philadelphia, attending sessions of Congress, and even visiting the Continental Army in the field. His energy was unflagging in the midst of personal hardship, including the death of one of his sons, who was killed at the battle of Germantown. But the end of the Revolution left the college in a shambles. Nassau Hall had been plundered by the British and Hessians, enrollment was down drastically, and so were the college's financial affairs.

During the Confederation period, Witherspoon set about rebuilding the college and reentered New Jersey politics. In 1787 he was a leader of the New Jersey ratifying convention and spearheaded the early ratification of the Constitution, which was unanimous. Following ratification, Witherspoon's health began to decline, though apparently not his vigor; after the death of his wife, he raised Princeton eyebrows by marrying a twenty-four-year-old widow who bore him two more children in his old age. As his eyesight failed along with his general health, Witherspoon turned over control of the college to his son-in-law Samuel Stanhope Smith, though the Old Doctor retained the title of president and some of its incumbent duties. John Witherspoon died at Princeton in 1794, having lived a life that suggests he be removed from the roll of Forgotten Founders.

Main Contributions of John Witherspoon

Witherspoon was the only active clergyman and college president to sign the Declaration of Independence.

Witherspoon had a direct hand in passing three of the four organic laws of the United States: the Declaration of Independence, the Articles of Confederation, and the Constitution.

As president and professor of moral philosophy at Princeton during the critical years of the Founding (1768–1794), Witherspoon helped produce the most important and impressive leadership generation in American history, including a U.S. president (James Madison, who stayed an extra term after graduation to be tutored by Witherspoon), a vice president, seventy-seven congressmen, and three Supreme Court justices, along with many state and local office holders.

From the Pen of John Witherspoon

Whereas, it hath pleased Almighty God, the father of mercies, remarkably to assist and support the United States of America in their important struggle for liberty, against the long continued efforts of a powerful nation: it is the duty of all ranks to observe and thankfully acknowledge the interpositions of his Providence in their behalf. Through the whole of the contest, from its first rise to this time, the influence of Divine Providence may be clearly perceived in many signal instances, of which we mention but a few.

In revealing the councils of our enemies, when the discoveries were seasonable and important, and the means seemingly inadequate or fortuitous; in preserving and even improving the union of the several States, on the breach of which our enemies placed their greatest dependence; in increasing the number and adding to the zeal and attachment of the friends of Liberty; in granting remarkable deliverances, and blessing us with the most signal success, when affairs seemed to have the most discouraging appearance; in raising up for us a powerful and generous ally, in one of the first of the European powers; in confounding the councils of our enemies, and suffering them to pursue such measures as have most directly contributed to frustrate their own desires and expectations; above all, in making their extreme cruelty to the inhabitants of these

States, when in their power, and their savage devastation of property, the very means of cementing our union, and adding vigor to every effort in opposition to them.

And as we cannot help leading the good people of these States to a retrospect on the events which have taken place since the beginning of the war, so we recommend in a particular manner to their observation, the goodness of God in the year now drawing to a conclusion; in which the Confederation of the United States has been completed, in which there have been so many instances of prowess and success in our armies; particularly in the Southern States, where, notwithstanding the difficulties with which they had to struggle, they have recovered the whole country which the enemy had overrun, leaving them only a post or two on or near the sea; in which we have been so powerfully and effectually assisted by our allies, while in all the conjunct operations the most perfect harmony has subsisted in the allied army; in which there has been so plentiful a harvest, and so great abundance of the fruits of the earth of every kind, as not only enables us easily to supply the wants of the army, but gives comfort and happiness to the whole people; and in which, after the success of our allies by sea, a General of the first Rank, with his whole army, has been captured by the allied forces under the direction of our Commander in Chief.

It is therefore recommended to the several states to set apart the thirteenth day of December next, to be religiously observed as a Day of Thanksgiving and Prayer; that all the people may assemble on that day, with grateful hearts, to celebrate the praise of our gracious Benefactor; to confess our manifold sins; to offer up our most fervent supplications to the God of all grace, that it may please Him to pardon our offences, and incline our hearts for the future to keep all his laws; to comfort and relieve all our brethren who are in distress or captivity; to prosper all husbandmen, and give success to all engaged in lawful commerce; to impart wisdom and integrity to our counsellors, judgment and fortitude to our officers and soldiers; to protect and prosper our illustrious ally, and favor our united exertions for the speedy establishment of a safe, honorable and lasting peace; and bless all seminaries of learning; and cause the knowledge of God to cover the earth, as the water covers the seas.

—John Witherspoon, Congressional Thanksgiving Day Proclamation (October 26, 1781)

Recommended Reading

Varnum Lansing Collins, *President Witherspoon: A Biography*, 2 vols. (Princeton: Princeton University Press, 1925; repr. New York: Arno Press, 1969).

Jeffry H. Morrison, *John Witherspoon and the Founding of the American Republic* (Notre Dame: University of Notre Dame Press, 2005).

L. Gordon Tait, *The Piety of John Witherspoon: Pew, Pulpit, and Public Forum* (Louisville: Geneva Press, 2001).

John Witherspoon, *The Selected Writings of John Witherspoon*, ed. Thomas Miller (Carbondale: Southern Illinois University Press, 1990).

CONCLUSION
America's *Other* Forgotten Founders

GARY L. GREGG II and MARK DAVID HALL

IT IS DIFFICULT TO IMAGINE A COURSE TODAY COVERING THE American Founding that does not consider the contributions of women and racial minorities. Because they were either formally or informally banned from holding political offices, it was harder for them to directly affect public policy. A burgeoning literature has demonstrated, however, that educated women often exercised significant personal influence or made a substantial impact through their writings. Participants in the first round of the survey suggested a number of women whom they believed should be remembered today, including Abigail Adams, Mercy Otis Warren, Dolley Payne Madison, Judith Sargent Murray, and Phillis Wheatley.

We were somewhat surprised that neither Abigail Adams nor Mercy Otis Warren was included among the top ten forgotten Founders (the top thirty list included Dolley Madison and Mercy Warren, but not Abigail Adams). We suspect that many respondents did not consider Abigail to be "forgotten." Scholars and popular authors alike have noted that she had a fine, penetrating mind and that she offered political advice to her husband. She is certainly well known for her March 1776 letter to John Adams, then serving in Congress, in which she advised:

> Remember the Ladies, and be more generous and favour-
> able to them than your ancestors. Do not put such unlimited
> power into the hands of the Husbands. Remember all Men
> would be tyrants if they could. If perticular care and attention
> is not paid to the Ladies we are determined to foment a Rebe-
> lion, and will not hold ourselves bound by any Laws in which
> we have no voice, or Representation.

Mercy Otis Warren is less well known than Abigail, but she was more directly involved in political debates through her public writings (although she often wrote under a pseudonym). Survey participant Carol Berkin observed that she was a "key propagan-dist for radicals in Massachusetts [and] wrote the first history of the Revolution." She also regularly corresponded with a range of political leaders, and in 1788 she published an essay entitled "Observations on the New Constitution," which argued against ratification of the proposed Constitution.

Adams and Warren were learned women who had immediate or indirect access to a range of American political leaders. One respondent, who declined to be identified or participate further in our study, suggested that "the forgotten Founders are: every Patriot woman who stayed home and took care of farms & families while their husbands and sons were away fighting in the Revolu-tionary War or serving overseas as a diplomat or in the Continental Congress."

We agree that these women, like their better known elite sis-ters, should not be forgotten.

Even more than white women, racial minorities in the Founding era were excluded from positions of public influence. But that did not mean that they did not contribute to America's Founding. One intriguing suggestion for approaching these Founders is to focus on a representative of a group. For instance, law professor William R. Casto suggested that Jack Arabas be included as an important forgotten Founder, explaining:

> I view Jack Arabas as a representative of the black soldiers who fought for America's freedom in the Revolutionary War. Arabas was a slave whose owner put him in the Connecticut Continental Line in 1777 in exchange for a bounty. When the war was over six years later, his owner reclaimed him. Jack ran off and was arrested as a runaway slave in New Haven. The Connecticut Superior Court, however, declared that Arabas's service made him a free man. He lived the rest of his life in New Haven.

Conversely, political science professor Alan Gibson proposed "Colonel Tye, the slave Titus, who fought with the British against the Revolutionaries. Most slaves who fought in the Revolution fought for the British. This is a very unrecognized aspect of the American Revolution." Ideally, it seems to us, both Arabas and Tye, or similar "representatives" of these groups, should be discussed in any course covering the Revolution.

Casto and Gibson gently challenged the individualistic bias of our survey, but Bruce Johansen more directly pointed out:

> Your form seems tailored to individual names, not a confederacy of nations such as the Iroquois. That being the case, I would select two Iroquois leaders. One was Canassatego, the Tadodaho

(speaker) of the Confederacy, who admonished the colonist to unite on a federal model as early as 1744. . . . Another Iroquois leader, whom the English call Hendrick (his Native name was Tiyanoga), was invited to the Albany Congress to advise the colonial delegates on how the Iroquois Confederacy operates.

We agree that the possible influence of the Iroquois on the American Founding is worthy of consideration, and we appreciate as well the comment made by Colin G. Calloway of Dartmouth College that students of the Founding should consider Native Americans such as Dragging Canoe, Cornstalk, White Eyes, and Nancy Ward, who are an important (and often sad) part of the story of the westward expansion of Americans of European descent.

Numerous survey participants suggested that ministers have been unjustly neglected in the study of the American Founding. John Witherspoon, it is true, made our list of top ten forgotten Founders, but we wonder if he would be on it if he had not been the only active clergyman to sign the Declaration of Independence. This event was certainly significant, but more important still were the thousands of sermons preached by Witherspoon, his contemporaries, and his predecessors that directly or indirectly encouraged Americans to protect their God-given rights, support government by consent of the governed, and guard against the concentration of power in the hands of sinful creatures. One of our respondents, Marvin Olasky, editor in chief of *WORLD*, contended:

> George Whitefield became a grandfather of the American Revolution when he argued that Christian subjects must obey divine laws and could, if necessary, break laws that pressed them to do wrong. . . . One of Whitefield's followers, Elisha

Williams, played out such thought at greater length in a pamphlet published in 1744 "The Essential Rights and Liberties of Protestants."

Other ministers suggested by respondents include Ezra Stiles, Samuel Miller, William White, David Griffith, Bishop James Madison, George Duffield, John Leland, Isaac Backus, and John and Frederick Muhlenberg.

Finally, a significant group about which many respondents were passionate was the Anti-Federalists. The Anti-Federalists consisted of a diverse group of political figures who, in general, opposed the concentration of power in a strong central government, supported vital state and local governments, advocated a clear articulation of rights, and opposed ratification of the proposed national constitution of 1787. In addition to the two Anti-Federalists who made our top ten list of forgotten Founders (George Mason and Patrick Henry), survey participants suggested, among others: (1) Richard Henry Lee, who, according to Howard L. Lubert, clearly belongs in the "pantheon of Founders" if he is the author of the "Federal Farmer." In a similar vein, Walter Nicgorski contended that Lee, "or whoever wrote the 'Federal Farmer,'" offered "intelligent and farseeing objections to the proposed Constitution, a match for Publius in his coherence and depth." (2) Robert Yates, who, according to Terence Ball, likely "became the pseudonymous 'Brutus,' who published an influential series of sixteen letters opposing ratification. Many of the pro-Constitution arguments and defenses offered by 'Publius' in the *Federalist Papers* are direct replies and responses to Brutus." Likewise, Gordon Lloyd wrote that Brutus's essays "are the best ever written that warned about the potential dangers of inadequate representation, the absence of a Bill of Rights, and the power of the judiciary in the original Constitution." (3) Melancton Smith, who, according to Ralph Ketcham, was the "most important Anti-Federalist theorist and spokesman." (4) Luther Martin, who, E. Christian Kopff argued, "was the most articulate and learned of the defenders of the rights and sovereignty of states." (5) John Taylor of Carolina, who, Garrett Ward Sheldon noted, was a "leading Anti-Federalist . . . [who] wrote extensively on constitutionalism, economics, agriculture, slavery, and rights."

We quote extensively (but not comprehensively) from supporters of different Anti-Federalists to help communicate how strongly many survey respondents thought their contributions to the creation of the American Republic have been neglected. As noted above, men and women on the "losing" side of history are often neglected by history texts, but at least among our respondents, there seems to be a consensus that the Anti-Federalists should be seriously considered in courses covering the Founding era.

CONCLUSION

The primary purpose of our survey and this book is to promote a broader discussion of America's Founding era. The survey reveals that there is a significant scholarly consensus that a number of important Founders have been unjustly neglected. Exploring the thoughts and actions of these men is a good place to begin a larger conversation. A robust and accurate treatment of America's Founders, however, must move beyond the fifteen or so men intimately involved in promoting the Revolution and Constitution to include the wide range of men and women who helped make America what it is today.

APPENDIX A
The Forgotten Founders:
The Complete List of Nominees

Roger Sherman

Edmund Randolph

James Wilson

Fisher Ames

George Mason

Francis Marion

John Dickinson

George Duffield

Gouverneur Morris

George Whitefield

John Witherspoon

George Wythe

John Jay

Isaac Backus

Melancton Smith

Jack Arabas

Richard Henry Lee

James Monroe

Oliver Ellsworth

John Allen

Benjamin Rush

John Carroll

James Iredell

John Lansing

James Otis

John Leland

Thomas Paine

John McDonald

Elbridge Gerry

John Ross

Luther Martin

John Rutledge of SC

Robert Yates

John Stuart

Bishop James Madison
John Taylor
"Brutus"
Joseph Brant
Dolley Payne Madison
Nancy Ward
Elias Boudinot
Nathaniel Macon
Elisha Williams
Pelatiah Webster
Ezra Stiles
Penelope Burke
Frederick Augustus Muhlenberg
Philip Freneau
John Marshall
Phillis Wheatley
Mercy Otis Warren
Robert Morris
Nathanael Greene
Samuel Langdon

Patrick Henry
Samuel Miller
Samuel Adams
Samuel Sherwood
Aaron Burr
Tench Coxe
Albert Gallatin
Theophilus Parsons
Anthony Benezet
White Eyes
Charles Pinckney
William Findley
Colonel Tye
William Paterson
Cornstalk
William Richardson Davie
David Griffith
William White
Dragging Canoe

APPENDIX B
The Forgotten Founders:
The Top Thirty Finalists

Rank	Name	Total Points
1	James Wilson	214
2	George Mason	152
3	Gouverneur Morris	128
4	John Jay	125
5	Roger Sherman	124
6	John Marshall	117
7	John Dickinson	92
8	Thomas Paine	76
9	Patrick Henry	71
10	John Witherspoon	68
11	Samuel Adams	66
12	Melancton Smith	55
13	Benjamin Rush	52
14	James Iredell	37
15	Oliver Ellsworth	36

Rank	Name	Total Points
16	Richard Henry Lee	34
17	James Otis	33
18	Elbridge Gerry	32
19	Luther Martin	31
20	Nathanael Greene	30
21	Fisher Ames (tie)	19
21	Robert Yates (tie)	19
23	Bishop James Madison	13
24	Elisha Williams (tie)	12
24	Dolley Paine Todd Madison (tie)	12
24	John Leland (tie)	12
27	Frederick Augustus Muhlenberg	6
28	Mercy Otis Warren	5
29	Elias Boudinot	4
30	Ezra Stiles	1

APPENDIX C

The Forty-Five Scholars Who Participated in the
Forgotten Founders Survey

HENRY J. ABRAHAM is James Hart Professor Emeritus of Government and Foreign Affairs at the University of Virginia. His numerous books include *Justices, Presidents, and Senators: A History of the U.S. Supreme Court Appointments from Washington to Bush II*; *Freedom and the Court: Civil Rights and Liberties in the United States*; and *The Judicial Process: An Introductory Analysis of the Courts of the United States, England, and France*. A pioneer in comparative judicial studies, Professor Abraham has served as a Fulbright Scholar in Denmark and has lectured throughout the world.

WILLIAM B. ALLEN is emeritus professor of political philosophy at Michigan State University. He has written or edited *George Washington: A Collection*; *Rethinking Uncle Tom: The Political Philosophy of Harriet Beecher Stowe*; *George Washington: America's First Progressive*; *The Personal and the Political: Three Fables of Montesquieu*; and *Habits of Mind: Fostering Access and Excellence in Higher Education* (with Carol M. Allen). Dr. Allen has served on the National Council for the Humanities and as member and chairman of the United States Commission on Civil Rights.

TERENCE BALL is professor of political science at Arizona State University. In addition to many articles in scholarly journals, he is the author of six books, including *Transforming Political Discourse: Political Theory and Crticial Conceptual History*; *Reappraising Political Theory: Revisionist Studies in the History of Political Thought*; and a mystery novel, *Rousseau's Ghost*. He has also edited or coedited eleven books, including *The Federalist* and the *Cambridge History of Twentieth-Century Political Thought*.

RYAN J. BARILLEAUX is professor of political science at Miami University (Ohio). He is the author or editor of numerous books and scholarly articles, including *The Post-Modern Presidency: The Office After Ronald Reagan*; *Presidential Frontiers: Underexplored Issues in White House Politics*; and *The Unitary Executive and the Modern Presidency* (with Christopher S. Kelley).

CAROL BERKIN is Presidential Professor of History at Baruch College and the Graduate Center, CUNY. Her publications include *Jonathan Sewall: Odyssey of an American Loyalist*; *First Generations: Women in Colonial America*; *A Brilliant Solution: Inventing the American Constitution*; *Revolutionary Mothers: Women in the Struggle for America's Independence*; and *Civil War Wives: The Life and Times of Angelina Grimké Weld, Varina Howell Davis, and Julia Dent Grant*. Dr. Berkin has also appeared as an onscreen commentator in the PBS series *New York* (by Ric Burns), in the MPH series *The Founding Fathers*, and in Middlemarch Productions' *Liberty! The American Revolution* and *Benjamin Franklin*.

R. B. BERNSTEIN is Distinguished Adjunct Professor of Law at New York Law School and the author or editor of nearly twenty volumes on American constitutional history. *Are We to Be a Nation?: The Making of the Constitution*; *Amending America: If We Love the Constitution So Much, Why Do We Keep Trying to Change It?*; and *Thomas Jefferson* were all nominated for the Pulitzer, Bancroft, and Parkman prizes. His recent book *The Founding Fathers Reconsidered* was a finalist for the George Washington Prize.

Thomas E. Buckley is professor of American religious history at the Jesuit School of Theology at Berkeley. Dr. Buckley's research interests are in the history of church-state relations with an emphasis on Thomas Jefferson's writings and the interaction of religion with government policy in the United States. He is the author of *Church and State in Revolutionary Virginia, 1776–1787* and *"The Great Catastrophe of My Life": Divorce in the Old Dominion*, and is the editor of *"If You Love That Lady Don't Marry Her": The Courtship Letters of Sally McDowell and John Miller, 1854–1856*. He is currently working on a study of the church-state relationship in Virginia from Jamestown to 1940.

Colin G. Calloway is John Kimball Jr. 1943 Professor of History and Professor of Native American Studies at Dartmouth College. He is the author of many books, including *The Indian History of an American Institution: Native Americans and Dartmouth*; *White People, Indians, and Highlanders: Tribal Peoples and Colonial Encounters in Scotland and America*; and *One Vast Winter Count: The Native American West before Lewis and Clark*, winner of the Caroline Bancroft History Prize.

William R. Casto is the Paul Whitfield Horn University Professor of Law at Texas Tech University. He has written numerous articles and three well-received books: *The Supreme Court in the Early Republic: The Chief Justiceships of John Jay and Oliver Ellsworth*; *Oliver Ellsworth and the Creation of the Federal Republic;* and *Foreign Affairs and the Constitution in the Age of Fighting Sail*.

H. Lee Cheek Jr. is dean of the School of Social Sciences and professor of political science and religion at Gainesville State College. His books include *Calhoun and Popular Rule: The Political Theory of the Disquisition and Discourse*; *Political Philosophy and Cultural Renewal*; and *Order and Legitimacy*. He is currently writing an intellectual biography of Francis Graham Wilson, a study of the American Founding, and a book on Patrick Henry's constitutionalism and political theory.

APPENDIX C

CHRISTOPHER COLLIER is professor emeritus of history at the Universities of Bridgeport and Connecticut. He was nominated for a Pulitzer Prize for his book *Roger Sherman's Connecticut: Yankee Politics and the American Revolution*. He also published *All Politics Is Local: Family, Friends, and Provincial Interests in the Creation of the Constitution* and, with James Lincoln Collier, *Decision in Philadelphia: The Constitutional Convention of 1787*. In addition, he wrote eight historical novels for young adults, a twenty-three-volume history of the United States for middle-school students, and many articles on the legal and constitutional history of the United States and Connecticut.

DANIEL L. DREISBACH is professor in the School of Public Affairs at American University in Washington, D.C. Professor Dreisbach's principal research interests include American constitutional law and history, First Amendment law, church-state relations, and criminal procedure. He has written extensively on these topics and has written or edited seven books, including *Thomas Jefferson and the Wall of Separation between Church and State*. He has published more than fifty book chapters, reviews, and articles in scholarly journals, including *American Journal of Legal History, Emory Law Journal, Journal of Church and State, North Carolina Law Review,* and *William and Mary Quarterly*.

MICHAEL P. FEDERICI is professor of political science at Mercyhurst College (Pennsylvania). A frequent contributor to scholarly journals, he is also the author of *The Challenge of Populism: The Rise of Right-Wing Democratism in Postwar America* and *Eric Voegelin: The Restoration of Order*. He is editor of a collection of Orestes Brownson's political writings (forthcoming) and is writing a book on the political theory of Alexander Hamilton.

MATTHEW J. FRANCK is director of the William E. and Carol G. Simon Center on Religion and the Constitution of the Witherspoon Institute in Princeton, New Jersey. He is professor emeritus of political science at Radford University in Virginia, where he taught constitutional law, American politics, and political philosophy. Franck is

172

the author of *Against the Imperial Judiciary: The Supreme Court vs. the Sovereignty of the People* and coeditor of *Sober as a Judge: The Supreme Court and Republican Liberty*. He is currently writing a book entitled *Strict Scrutiny: Sense and Nonsense on the Supreme Court*.

BRUCE FROHNEN is associate professor of law at Ohio Northern University and senior fellow at the Russell Kirk Center for Cultural Renewal. He is the author or editor of many books, including *Virtue and the Promise of Conservatism: The Legacy of Burke and Tocqueville*; *The New Communitarians and the Crisis of Modern Liberalism*; *The American Republic: Primary Sources*; *The Anti-Federalists: Selected Writings and Speeches*; and *Community and Tradition: Conservative Perspectives on the American Experience* (with George W. Carey).

RICHARD M. GAMBLE is Anna Margaret Ross Alexander Professor of History and Political Science and associate professor of history at Hillsdale College. His essays and reviews have appeared in the *Journal of Southern History, Orbis, Humanitas*, the *Intercollegiate Review*, and the *Independent Review*. He is the author of *The War for Righteousness: Progressive Christianity, the Great War, and the Rise of the Messianic Nation* and editor of *The Great Tradition: Classic Readings on What It Means to Be an Educated Human Being*.

SCOTT DOUGLAS GERBER holds the Ella and Ernest Chair in Law and is professor of law in the Claude W. Pettit College of Law at Ohio Northern University. Dr. Gerber is also senior research scholar in law and politics at the Social Philosophy and Policy Center. He has published six books and nearly one hundred articles, book reviews, op-eds, and sundry pieces.

ALAN GIBSON is professor of political science at California State University–Chico. His teaching and research interests focus on the political thought of James Madison and the study of the American Founding. He has published articles in *Polity, History of Political Thought*, the *Review of Politics*, and the *Political Science Reviewer*. Most recently, Dr. Gibson is the author of two books on the historiography of the

American Founding: *Interpreting the Founding: Guide to the Enduring Debates over the Origins and Foundations of the American Republic* and *Understanding the Founding: The Crucial Questions.*

DAVID L. HOLMES is Walter G. Mason Professor of Religious Studies at the College of William and Mary. He is the author of *A Brief History of Episcopal Church*; *A Nation Mourns*; and *The Faiths of the Founding Fathers*. Dr. Holmes has also written numerous articles.

RALPH KETCHAM is professor emeritus of citizenship and public affairs at the Maxwell School, Syracuse University. His books include *Benjamin Franklin*; *Framed for Posterity: The Enduring Philosophy of the Constitution*; and *The Idea of Democracy in the Modern Era.*

E. CHRISTIAN KOPFF is associate director of the Honors Program and director of the Center for Western Civilization at the University of Colorado, Boulder. He is editor of a critical edition of the Greek text of Euripides' *Bacchae* and author of more than one hundred articles and reviews on scholarly, pedagogical, and popular topics. He also wrote *The Devil Knows Latin: Why America Needs the Classical Tradition*, which is widely cited in the new classical education movement.

RALPH LERNER is the Benjamin Franklin Professor Emeritus at the University of Chicago and professor in the Committee on Social Thought at the University of Chicago. Among his publications are the award-winning article "Commerce and Character: The Anglo-American as New-Model Man" and the books *The Thinking Revolutionary: Principle and Practice in the New Republic* and *Revolutions Revisited: Two Faces of the Politics of Enlightenment.*

MICHAEL LIENESCH is professor of American political thought in the department of political science at the University of North Carolina at Chapel Hill. His books include *New Order of the Ages: Time, the Constitution, and the Making of Modern American Political Thought*; *Ratifying the Constitution*; and *In the Beginning: Fundamentalism, the Scopes Trial, and the Making of the Antievolution Movement.*

GORDON LLOYD is professor of policy in the Graduate School of Public Policy at Pepperdine University in Malibu, California. He has written and lectured extensively on the moral and intellectual foundations of political economy, particularly with respect to the fate of classical liberalism. Dr. Lloyd is coeditor of *The Essential Antifederalist* and *The Essential Bill of Rights: Original Arguments and Documents*.

ROBERT D. LOEVY is professor of political science at Colorado College, where he has taught since 1968. Specializing in presidency studies and civil rights, he is the author of numerous books, including *Flawed Path to the Presidency: Unfairness and Inequality in the Presidential Selection Process* and *The Manipulated Path to the White House 1996: Maximizing Advantage in the Presidential Selection Process*.

HOWARD L. LUBERT is associate professor of political science at James Madison University, where he teaches the introductory course in political theory as well as upper-level courses in American political thought, and humor and politics. He is coeditor of *Classics of American Political and Constitutional Thought* (2 vols.) and *The Debate over Slavery in the United States, 1776–1865* (forthcoming). He has also written various articles on eighteenth-century political thought, including "Sovereignty and Liberty in William Blackstone's Commentaries on the Laws of England" in *Review of Politics* and "Jonathan Mayhew: Conservative Revolutionary" in *History of Political Thought* (forthcoming).

PAULINE MAIER is William R. Kenan Jr. Professor of American History at the Massachusetts Institute of Technology. Her books include *From Resistance to Revolution: Colonial Radicals and the Development of American Opposition to Britain, 1765–1776*; *The Old Revolutionaries: Political Lives in the Age of Samuel Adams*; and *American Scripture: Making the Declaration of Independence*. She is also coauthor of the American history textbook *Inventing America*.

MICHAEL W. MCCONNELL is Richard and Frances Mallery Professor of Law at Stanford University, director of Stanford Constitutional

Law Center, and senior fellow at the Hoover Institution. Previously he was a judge on the U.S. Court of Appeals for the Tenth Circuit. He is author of numerous articles and coauthor of two casebooks: *The Constitution of the United States* and *Religion and the Constitution*.

WILFRED M. MCCLAY is professor of history and holds the SunTrust Bank Chair of Excellence in the Humanities at the University of Tennessee at Chattanooga. His book *The Masterless: Self and Society in Modern America* won the 1995 Merle Curti Award in Intellectual History, which is awarded by the Organization of American Historians.

JEFFRY H. MORRISON is associate professor of government at Regent University and a faculty member at the federal government's James Madison Foundation in Washington, D.C. He has written two books, *John Witherspoon and the Founding of the American Republic* and *The Political Philosophy of George Washington*, and is coeditor of *The Founders on God and Government* and *The Forgotten Founders on Religion and Public Life*.

WALTER NICGORSKI is professor in the Program of Liberal Studies and concurrent professor of political science at the University of Notre Dame. His articles have appeared in numerous journals, including *Political Theory, Interpretation,* the *Review of Politics,* and the *Political Science Reviewer.* He coedited and contributed to *An Almost Chosen People: The Moral Aspirations of Americans* and *Leo Strauss: Political Philosopher and Jewish Thinker.*

MARVIN OLASKY is a senior fellow at the Acton Institute for the Study of Religion and Liberty. He is the editor in chief of *WORLD,* a national weekly newsmagazine from a biblical perspective. He has written twenty books on history and cultural analysis, including *Compassionate Conservatism: What It Is, What It Does, and How It Can Transform; The American Leadership Tradition: Moral Vision from Washington to Clinton; The Tragedy of American Compassion; Fighting for Liberty and Virtue: Political and Cultural Wars in Eighteenth-Century America;* and *Abortion Rights.*

BARBARA A. PERRY is a senior fellow in the Presidential Oral History Program at the University of Virginia's Miller Center of Public Affairs. Previously, she was the Carter Glass Professor of Government and founding director of the Center for Civic Renewal at Sweet Briar College. Her books include *"The Supremes": An Introduction to the U.S. Supreme Court Justices*; *The Michigan Affirmative Action Cases*; *Jacqueline Kennedy: First Lady of the New Frontier*; *Freedom and the Court: Civil Rights and Liberties in the United States*, eighth edition (with Henry J. Abraham); *The Priestly Tribe: The Supreme Court's Image in the American Mind*; *Civil Liberties Under the Constitution*, sixth edition (with M. Glenn Abernathy); *A "Representative" Supreme Court? The Impact of Race, Religion, and Gender on Appointments*; and *Unfounded Fears: Myths and Realities of a Constitutional Convention* (with Paul J. Weber).

SAIKRISHNA PRAKASH is David Lurton Massee Jr. Professor of Law and Sullivan & Cromwell Professor of Law at the University of Virginia. A former law clerk at the U.S. Supreme Court, he has published articles on issues concerning executive power and federalism, which have appeared in numerous law journals, including *Yale Law Journal*, *Virginia Law Review*, *Columbia Law Review*, *Chicago Law Review*, and *Texas Law Review*.

STEPHEN B. PRESSER is Raoul Berger Professor of Legal History at Northwestern University School of Law. A renowned constitutional law scholar, he has frequently testified before the U.S. House of Representatives. He is the author or coauthor of numerous articles and books, including *The Original Misunderstanding: The English, the Americans, and the Dialectic of Federalist Jurisprudence* and *The American Constitutional Order: Introduction to the History and Nature of American Constitutional Law* (with Douglas W. Kmiec).

ELLIS SANDOZ is Hermann Moyse Jr. Distinguished Professor of Political Science and director of the Eric Voegelin Institute for American Renaissance Studies at Louisiana State University. His publications include *Republicanism, Religion, and the Soul of America*;

Political Apocalypse: A Study of Dostoevsky's "Grand Inquisitor"; and *A Government of Laws: Political Theory, Religion, and the American Founding.* He is also the general editor of *The Collected Works of Eric Voegelin* (34 vols., University of Missouri Press).

COLLEEN A. SHEEHAN is associate professor of political science at Villanova University and Director of the Matthew J. Ryan Center for the Study of Free Institutions and the Public Good. Her publications include *James Madison and the Spirit of Republican Self-Government*; "The Commerce of Ideas and Cultivation of Character in Madison's Republic" in Bradley C. S. Watson, ed., *Civic Education and Culture*; "Madison v. Hamilton: The Battle Over Republicanism and the Role of Public Opinion" in *American Political Science Review*; and "Madison and the French Enlightenment: The Authority of Public Opinion" in *William and Mary Quarterly.*

GARRETT WARD SHELDON is John Morton Beaty Professor of Political and Social Sciences at the University of Virginia's College at Wise. His publications include *The Political Philosophy of James Madison*; *The Political Philosophy of Thomas Jefferson*; *The Liberal Republicanism of John Taylor of Caroline* (with C. William Hill Jr.); and *Encyclopedia of Political Thought.*

DAVID J. SIEMERS is assistant professor of political science at the University of Wisconsin–Osh Kosh. Dr. Siemers's research interests include American political thought and the U.S. presidency. He is the author of *Ratifying the Republic: Antifederalists and Federalists in Constitutional Time.*

C. BRADLEY THOMPSON is BB&T Research Professor at Clemson University and the executive director of the Clemson Institute for the Study of Capitalism. His publications include *Anti-Slavery Political Writings, 1833–1860: A Reader*; *The Revolutionary Writings of John Adams*; and *John Adams and the Spirit of Liberty.*

GARRY WILLS is professor of history emeritus at Northwestern University. His numerous books have won many awards—the Pulitzer Prize among them. He has received nineteen honorary doctorates.

THOMAS G. WEST is professor of politics at the University of Dallas. He is also a director and senior fellow of the Claremont Institute. He is the author of *Vindicating the Founders: Race, Sex, Class, and Justice in the Origins of America.*

CHRISTOPHER WOLFE is emeritus professor of political science at Marquette University, vice president of the Thomas International project, and codirector of the Ralph McInerny Center for Thomistic Studies. His books include *Judicial Activism: Bulwark of Freedom or Precarious Security?*; *How to Read the Constitution: Originalism, Constitutional Interpretation, and Judicial Power*; and *Natural Law Liberalism.*

JEAN M. YARBROUGH is professor of government and Gary M. Pendy Sr. Professor of Social Sciences at Bowdoin College. She is the author of *American Virtues: Thomas Jefferson on the Character of a Free People* and editor of *The Essential Jefferson.* She has written numerous articles and serves on the editorial board of the *Review of Politics* and *Polity.* She is currently completing a study of Theodore Roosevelt and a Progressive critique of the Founders.

MICHAEL P. ZUCKERT is Nancy Reeves Dreux Professor of Political Science at the University of Notre Dame. He has published numerous books, including *Natural Rights and the New Republicanism*; *The Natural Rights Republic: Studies in the Foundation of the American Political Tradition*; and *The Truth About Leo Strauss: Political Philosophy and American Democracy* (with Catherine Zuckert). He has written articles on a variety of topics, including George Orwell, Plato's *Apology*, Shakespeare, and contemporary liberal theory.

APPENDIX D
About the Contributors

HENRY J. ABRAHAM is James Hart Professor Emeritus of Government and Foreign Affairs at the University of Virginia. His numerous books include *Justices, Presidents, and Senators: A History of the U.S. Supreme Court Appointments from Washington to Bush II*; *Freedom and the Court: Civil Rights and Liberties in the United States*; and *The Judicial Process: An Introductory Analysis of the Courts of the United States, England, and France*. A pioneer in comparative judicial studies, Professor Abraham has served as a Fulbright Scholar in Denmark and has lectured throughout the world.

JOHN K. BUSH, a graduate of Vanderbilt University and Harvard Law School, practices law in the Louisville office of Greenebaum, Doll & McDonald PLLC. He is currently writing a book about Gouverneur Morris.

DANIEL L. DREISBACH is professor in the School of Public Affairs at American University in Washington, D.C. Professor Dreisbach's principal research interests include American constitutional law and history, First Amendment law, church-state relations, and criminal procedure. He has written extensively on these topics and has written or edited seven books, including *Thomas Jefferson and the Wall of Separation between Church and State*. He has published more than fifty book chapters, reviews, and articles in scholarly journals, including *American Journal of Legal History, Emory Law Journal, Journal of Church and State, North Carolina Law Review*, and *William and Mary Quarterly*.

GARY L. GREGG II holds the Mitch McConnell Chair in Leadership at the University of Louisville, where he is also director of the McConnell Center. He is the author or editor of nine books, including *The Presidential Republic: Executive Representation and Deliberative Democracy*; *Securing Democracy: Why We Have an Electoral College*; and *Thinking about the Presidency: Documents and Essays from the Founding to the Present*. He is also author of a new fiction series for young adult readers called *The Remnant Chronicles*, the first two books of which have been published as *The Sporran* and *The Iona Conspiracy*.

MARK DAVID HALL is Herbert Hoover Distinguished Professor of Politics at George Fox University. He has written or coedited *The Political and Legal Philosophy of James Wilson, 1742–1798*; *The Founders on God and Government*; *The Collected Works of James Wilson* (2 vols.); *The Forgotten Founders on Religion and Public Life*; and *The Sacred Rights of Conscience: Selected Readings on Religious Liberty and Church-State Relations in the American Founding*. He is at work on *Roger Sherman and the Creation of the American Republic* and is coediting (with Daniel L. Dreisbach) *Faith and the Founders of the American Republic*, both forthcoming from Oxford University Press.

JONATHAN DEN HARTOG is assistant professor of history at Northwestern College (St. Paul, Minnesota). A specialist in American political and religious history, he received his doctorate from the University of Notre Dame in 2006. He is currently working on a book manuscript examining the religious dimension of Federalist Party politics.

THOMAS S. KIDD teaches history and is senior fellow at the Institute for Studies of Religion at Baylor University. He is the author of *Patrick Henry: First among Patriots*; *American Christians and Islam: Evangelical Culture and Muslims from the Colonial Period to the Age of Terrorism*; *The Great Awakening: The Roots of Evangelical Christianity in Colonial America*; *The Protestant Interest: New England after Puritanism*; and *God of Liberty: A Religious History of the American Revolution*. He is currently writing a biography of Patrick Henry.

HOWARD L. LUBERT is associate professor of political science at James Madison University, where he teaches the introductory course in political theory as well as upper-level courses in American political thought, and humor and politics. He is coeditor of *Classics of American Political and Constitutional Thought* (2 vols.) and *The Debate over Slavery in the United States, 1776–1865* (forthcoming). He has also written various articles on eighteenth-century political thought, including "Sovereignty and Liberty in William Blackstone's Commentaries on the Laws of England" in *Review of Politics*, and "Jonathan Mayhew: Conservative Revolutionary" in *History of Political Thought* (forthcoming).

JEFFRY H. MORRISON is associate professor of government at Regent University and a faculty member at the federal government's James Madison Foundation in Washington, D.C. He has written two books, *John Witherspoon and the Founding of the American Republic* and *The Political Philosophy of George Washington*, and he is coeditor of *The Founders on God and Government* and *The Forgotten Founders on Religion and Public Life*.

BARBARA A. PERRY is a senior fellow in the Presidential Oral History Program at the University of Virginia's Miller Center of Public Affairs. Previously, she was the Carter Glass Professor of Government and founding director of the Center for Civic Renewal at Sweet Briar College. Her books include *"The Supremes": An Introduction to the U.S. Supreme Court Justices*; *The Michigan Affirmative Action Cases*; *Jacqueline Kennedy: First Lady of the New Frontier*; *Freedom and the*

Court: Civil Liberties in the United States, eighth edition (with Henry J. Abraham); *The Priestly Tribe: The Supreme Court's Image in the American Mind*; *Civil Rights and Liberties Under the Constitution*, sixth edition (with M. Glenn Abernathy); *A "Representative" Supreme Court? The Impact of Race, Religion, and Gender on Appointments*; and *Unfounded Fears: Myths and Realities of a Constitutional Convention* (with Paul J. Weber).

DAVID J. VOELKER is associate professor of humanistic studies and history at the University of Wisconsin–Green Bay. He has written various essays on the politics, religion, and culture of the early American Republic.

ACKNOWLEDGMENTS

AS IN ANY SUCH ENDEAVOR, THE EDITORS HAVE NUMEROUS PEOPLE to whom we owe our gratitude. First, there are all those men and women, distinguished scholars all, who took the time to complete our survey and respond to our questions. Their names and brief biographies are found in Appendix C. Unless otherwise noted, all quotes about the forgotten Founders in this book come from these scholars.

We are particularly grateful to our colleagues who agreed to write chapters under an extremely tight deadline to help our readers learn more about the extraordinary accomplishments of those identified as our top ten greatest Founders who have been largely forgotten. To all of these men and women, we owe a considerable debt.

The survey itself would not have been possible if it were not for the diligent and good work of a number of staff and students at the McConnell Center who aided in the project. Derek Jones, Malana Salyer, Neil Salyer, Maria Teresa dela Cruz, Mary Kate Lindsey, Christopher McCloskey, and Laura Hunzinger all deserve our appreciation. For twenty years the McConnell Center has worked to nurture outstanding young people and bring the lessons of the Founding of the Republic to new generations. The center is part of the University of Louisville and sponsored both our survey and the original publication of this volume in 2008.

Most significantly, we need to recognize the accomplishments of the forgotten Founders profiled in this volume, and the men and women who gave their lives, shed their blood, and toiled with their minds and pens to create the American Republic. We owe them much. The least we can do is remember, and we hope this project will help us pay that debt.